The BRICS and the Financing Mechanisms They Created

The BRICS and the Financing Mechanisms They Created

Progress and Shortcomings

Paulo Nogueira Batista Jr.

ANTHEM PRESS

Anthem Press
An imprint of Wimbledon Publishing Company
www.anthempress.com

This edition first published in UK and USA 2022
by ANTHEM PRESS
75–76 Blackfriars Road, London SE1 8HA, UK
or PO Box 9779, London SW19 7ZG, UK
and
244 Madison Ave #116, New York, NY 10016, USA

British Library Cataloguing-in-Publication Data
A catalogue record for this book is available from the British Library.

Library of Congress Control Number: 2021946884

ISBN-13: 978-1-83998-206-4 (Hbk)
ISBN-10: 1-83998-206-3 (Hbk)

This title is also available as an e-book.

CONTENTS

A BRIEF NOTE

Paulo Nogueira Batista Jr. is a former executive director at the IMF in Washington DC for Brazil and other countries (2007–15), Brazilian delegate at G20 meetings (2007–14), Brazilian delegate at BRICS meetings and negotiations (2008–15), and vice president of the New Development Bank in Shanghai (2015–17).

This book is based on a paper prepared for the Global Development Policy Center of Boston University that was concluded in November 2020 and updated in January 2021. The views expressed are solely those of the author.

Chapter 1

INTRODUCTION

The BRICS formation—Brazil, Russia, India, China, and South Africa—has been operating since 2008 on a continuous basis and became early on a permanent and widely recognized feature of the international political and economic landscape. This was hardly surprising since it comprises five of the most important emerging market countries. The four original members, together with the United States, are among the group of only five countries that are on the lists of 10 largest territories, populations, and GDPs of the world.[1] South Africa, which joined the group in 2011, is one of the most important countries in sub-Saharan Africa.

This book begins with an overview of the BRICS as a cooperation mechanism from 2008 to the present days, examining its strong points and weaknesses. Emphasis is placed on economic and financial aspects, and especially on international governance issues, one of the most important original reasons for the creation of the BRICS. The overview describes how the BRICS were formed, their common traits, and challenges that arose during coordination efforts among the four and later five countries, including disclosure of episodes that illustrate the nature of the difficulties we encountered along the way. BRICS coordination in the IMF and some observations on the future of the group are also provided in the book, against the background of a world fractured by geopolitical tensions, and marked by the crisis of multilateralism, growing concerns with climate challenges, and the pandemic of 2020.

Since its creation 12 years ago, the BRICS have gone through different phases. Viewed from the angle of financial cooperation—the one adopted in this book—three broad phases can be distinguished. In the first phase, from 2008 to 2011, the BRICS focused mainly on working together in the G20, the IMF, and the World Bank to attempt to bring about a reform of the international financial architecture, and especially of the Bretton Woods institutions. This seemed to work well initially with the displacement of the G7 by the G20 as the main forum for international economic and financial

1. GDPs in purchasing power parity (PPP) terms.

cooperation and given the commitments made at the G20 to reform the IMF and the World Bank. Some progress was made in the IMF, notably in the 2010 quota and governance reform. By 2011 or even earlier, however, it became clear to the BRICS that progress in the Washington institutions would be slow and patchy. Americans and Europeans showed great reluctance to relinquish their privileged positions in the IMF and the World Bank. Allowing a truly decisive increase in the role of the BRICS and other emerging market and developing nations in the IMF and the World Bank was something they were not really ready to contemplate.

Without abandoning efforts, at least not at first, to reform the Bretton Woods institutions, the BRICS moved to create their own financing mechanisms in parallel. Naturally, both objectives were perfectly compatible, given that the creation of new mechanisms was aimed in part at increasing our leverage in the reform of the international financial architecture. Phase 2 of the BRICS process, from 2012 to 2014, corresponds to the negotiation between the five countries, at times exceedingly difficult, of a development bank and a monetary fund. The negotiations were eventually successful and the treaties creating the development bank and the monetary fund of the BRICS were signed during the Fortaleza BRICS Summit in Brazil, in July 2014. Ratification and approval by Parliaments or other State bodies occurred quickly and a year later, at the Ufa Summit in Russia, in July 2015, the BRICS Leaders could announce that the two financial mechanisms were entering into force.

Phase 3, from 2015 to the present day, corresponds to the implementation of these financial initiatives. I will argue that this implementation has largely been a disappointment so far. The monetary fund was held back by the conservatism of some of the central banks of the BRICS, notably of Brazil, that were somewhat frightened at the prospect of committing reserves to mutual support. The development bank was hampered partly by bad choices made by the countries for the first administration but perhaps chiefly by political developments that undermined the quality and strength of the BRICS process. I refer mainly to political developments in Brazil, since 2016 and especially since 2019, that undermined the country's commitment to the BRICS, and to the increasing conflicts between China and India, leading to skirmishes on the border in 2017 and again in 2020. The conflict between Russia and the West over Ukraine and Crimea also had negative spillovers for the BRICS, specifically for the multilateral development bank they created.

The book will address the main features of the financing institutions or mechanisms created by the BRICS in response to the difficulties in moving forward with the reform of the Bretton Woods institutions. As mentioned, two financing mechanisms were created by the BRICS: a monetary fund, named the BRICS Contingent Reserve Arrangement (CRA), and the New

Development Bank (NDB), commonly known as the BRICS bank. I will cover the complicated negotiations between the BRICS countries from 2012 to 2014, as well as the first five years of existence of the CRA and the NDB since the entry into force of the treaties signed in Fortaleza. The book deals more with the development bank than with the monetary fund, the NDB being the more important of the two.

What follows is based essentially on my practical experience with the BRICS process, initially as executive director at the IMF in Washington, DC, and as Brazilian delegate to the G20 and BRICS meetings. Subsequently, from 2012 to 2014, I was a participant for Brazil in the negotiations that led to the establishment of the CRA and the NDB. I worked especially on the former. Then I moved to China to become one of the founding members of the NDB. From July 2015 to October 2017, I held the position of Brazilian vice president of the NDB, headquartered in Shanghai. Thus, for most of the period covered by this book what is here presented is an insider's account of the BRICS process and of the CRA and NDB—a reexamination, with the benefit of hindsight, of what was accomplished, as well as the limitations and shortcomings of the progress we were able to make. A lot was achieved, as I will show, and if a negative tone prevails here and there, this is perhaps due to the fact that results are being assessed against the high aspirations that people like me—the "idealists" so to speak—pursued when we started out on this journey in 2008.

This book is based on a paper originally prepared for the Global Development Policy Center of Boston University. A number of people read and criticized preliminary versions. I thank Chris Humphrey, Gustavo Tavares da Costa, Pedro Fachada, Danny Bradlow, Kevin Gallagher and, especially, Sergio Xavier Ferreira, Greg Chin, Jonnas Esmeraldo de Vasconcelos, Aleksei Mozhin, and Hector Torres for corrections, comments, and suggestions, with the usual caveat that the responsibility for views expressed and remaining errors and omissions is mine exclusively. What the reader will find in this book is a mixture of analysis—economic, of international relations, and multilateral organizations—with narratives of negotiation processes, highlighting occasionally backstage incidents and controversies that are revealing of the nature of the BRICS grouping and of the stance taken by the participating countries. The book is based mostly on official documents (including many that were not publicly available, but that I have now posted on my webpage), my own personal notes and recollections from the period 2008 to 2017, as well as the notes and recollections of some people that shared these experiences of the BRICS process and were willing to convey them to me on occasion of the preparation and review of this book.

Chapter 2

THE BRICS COME TOGETHER

The BRICS were greeted initially with considerable skepticism in some quarters. At first sight, these countries seemed indeed to have little in common. Critics and skeptics were often adamant in pointing out what they believed to be the artificiality of the group, seen by some as merely a Goldman Sachs invention to market investments in the four original members. These doubts were legitimate. Who could deny the enormous differences between the countries—historical, political, economic, and cultural? In practical terms, could these countries really act together in any meaningful way? After all, what did Brazil have in common with Russia, or China with India, or India with Russia?

Coordination problems were undoubtedly very real, and I experienced them firsthand from the very beginning of the process in 2008. Nonetheless, it soon became clear that the BRICS cooperation mechanism had strong potential.

When I came to Washington DC, in 2007, to take up the position of executive director for Brazil and other Latin American and Caribbean countries in the IMF, the BRICS did not exist at all as a political reality. The quota and voice reform concluded in March, for example, whatever its merits, owes nothing to BRICS coordination. At the time, BRICS was indeed a mere acronym created by Jim O'Neill, an economist with Goldman Sachs. But O'Neill had hit on something not only economically but also politically significant.

The process began at the initiative of Russia. Russian officials, at different levels and places, approached their Brazilian, Chinese, and Indian counterparts and proposed that we coordinate our actions, focusing initially on economic and financial matters, and especially international governance issues. This happened in the IMF, the World Bank, at the G20, and in the capitals through Finance and Foreign Ministry channels. The Russian proposal was well received by the three other countries and coordination efforts started right away. South Africa would join later, in 2011.[1]

---

1. It should be noted that before South Africa joined in 2011 the acronym, as created by O'Neill, was BRICs, comprising the initial letters of the four original members. When

There are other versions, I note in passing, of how the BRICS began, including in Brazil, with former Brazilian officials claiming that the proposal came from them or jointly from Russia and Brazil. Success has many fathers, as the saying goes. But these versions have no correspondence with reality. It all began with Russia. So much so that the first BRICS Leaders' Summit was held in Ekaterinburg, in Russia, in June 2009.

Again, coordination problems were always daunting, reflecting divergent interests, differences in economic size, structure, and political or cultural realities. The four, later five, countries nevertheless showed a clear determination to overcome these divergences and differences—at least until recently. An indication of this political reality is the fact that the Leaders of the countries have met regularly once a year, since 2009, at their annual Summits. Moreover, since 2011, another tradition was created, at the initiative of Brazil, for the five Leaders to also meet informally at the margins of the G20 Summit, taking advantage of the fact that the BRICS are also G20 members. This began in Cannes, at the G20 Summit of the French presidency, in November 2011, and has continued since then. In Los Cabos, at the margin of the G20 Summit of the Mexican presidency, in June 2012, the BRICS Leaders began issuing written statements also at these so-called informal meetings. They have done so ever since.

From Cannes onward, the BRICS Leaders have met regularly twice a year, and insofar as I know, never has any of them missed these biannual encounters. This goes even for recent Brazilian presidents, Michel Temer (2016–18) and Jair Bolsonaro (since 2019), with weaker commitment to the BRICS—especially Bolsonaro, who eagerly sought alignment with President Donald Trump.

This brief description of the origins and initial phase of the BRICS does not capture the difficulties, hardship, and uncertainties that the process entailed for those directly involved. We had to struggle on an ongoing basis to achieve meaningful results. Many different types of barriers had to be overcome.

China, for example, the largest of the BRICS, could not always be expected to support or even to strictly abide by common positions. Countries have their national agendas, and this was to some extent true of all the BRICS, but more clearly so in the case of China. The Chinese were always under the temptation to strike an individual path, even at the cost of weakening the BRICS. They saw themselves as *primus inter pares* and had of course factual basis for this view. But there was also another element: incredible as this may seem in retrospect,

---

South Africa came in, the acronym became BRICS, with the capital S standing for the new member. I will ignore this slight complication in this book and use the acronym BRICS for the whole period, including before South Africa's entry.

given all that happened to US/China relations during the Trump presidency, China often seemed to harbor the hope that it could, given its unique size and importance, construct some sort of special relation with the United States and other Western powers, sacrificing to some extent, if needed, BRICS cooperation in the process. Something, however, protected the other BRICS from this risk: American reluctance (even during the Obama presidency), as well as European reluctance, to accept China as an equal and trustworthy partner.

BRICS coordination in the IMF

Even so, China tried repeatedly. In the IMF, for instance, the Brazilian, Russian, and Indian chairs worked closely together from 2008 onward. But we had to struggle to keep the Chinese chair more or less in line, meaning that, depending on the personality of the Chinese representatives, we sometimes came up against the country's excessive alignment to the positions of IMF management—positions that, more often than not, reflected those of the US Treasury. Moreover, the Chinese executive director and other officials were tightly controlled by the capital and responded slowly to coordination efforts. Beijing seemed to be often attracted by the possibility of side deals (e.g., positions for Chinese nationals in the IMF's senior administration or largely symbolic matters, such as the inclusion of the renminbi in the SDR basket[2]). Americans and Europeans sensed this and exploited these divisions to weaken the BRICS.

Nonetheless, BRICS coordination became in this period a recognized feature in the IMF Executive Board. Perhaps with some exaggeration, Aleksei Mozhin, the Russian executive director who had been in the institution for almost 20 years, went so far as to say that the emergence of the BRICS had been the most important change in IMF governance since his arrival in Washington, DC.

My former colleague may have overstated our importance, but I have no doubt that BRICS cooperation in the Executive Board became indeed very significant from 2008 onward. And I could always count on Aleksei Mozhin and, in the Indian chair, on Arvind Virmani and later Rakesh Mohan to play an active and sometimes leading role in many matters that came for Board

2. China was eventually successful on both counts. The renminbi was included in the SDR basket in 2016 and Beijing managed to secure a seemingly permanent position of deputy managing director for a Chinese national in the IMF administration, suggesting that its strategy of playing more or less by the rulebook, while not altering fundamentally the balance of power within the institution, paid off for China, at least for the short term.

consideration or decision. In the Chinese chair, He Jianxiong also had an important participation in our coordination efforts, despite tight control from Beijing. On many topics, especially policy issues, our five chairs worked more or less *in tandem* and achieved important results: for instance, on the discussion of capital flow management measures, or in the prolonged debates on quota formula and quota reform, or on lending to the IMF and in the review and actual operation of the New Arrangements to Borrow, where the BRICS managed to obtain veto power. After 2015, with the weakening of Brazil, due to the country's economic and political crisis, and also because of my own departure to Shanghai and Rakesh Mohan's subsequent replacement in the Indian chair, BRICS coordination in the IMF seems to have died away, despite Mozhin's continuing efforts. BRICS coordination in the World Bank had never been strong, even in the heyday of the BRICS, and remained lackluster or nonexistent after that.

BRICS excessively cautious, Brazil often the main engine

The BRICS, with the exception perhaps of Brazil up to 2014/2015, were sometimes excessively cautious and deferential in their relations with the United States and Europe. Even China, strange as it may seem in retrospect. In the initial years, it was not all easy, for example, to convene meetings of the BRICS Leaders on the sidelines of the G20 Summits. Officials from some of the countries seemed to feel that this would be seen by the advanced countries as hostile to the G20 process. Were it not for the determination of the Brazilian president, Dilma Rousseff, who valued the BRICS process, the practice would not have started at all, as it did in Cannes at the end of 2011.

It may be useful to briefly recap how this meeting came about in Cannes and the difficulties, sometimes apparently trivial, that we had to overcome to make things happen. At the time, the Brazilians were the ones attempting to convince the other four countries to hold an informal meeting of the BRICS Leaders. A rather ridiculous obstacle arose, however. It looked to me as more of a pretext than a real reason. In any case, the outgoing presidency of the BRICS process, China in 2011, and the incoming presidency, India in 2012, disagreed as to who should call the meeting. India wanted China to do it, China insisted that it was up to India. As the G20 Summit approached, this impasse seemed unsurmountable and at one point Brazilian diplomats were ready to give up.

Now, for the benefit of non-Brazilian readers, I should mention that President Dilma Rousseff was famous in Brazil not only for her strong and courageous personality but also for her lack of patience and diplomatic ability. As she arrived in Cannes and was informed of the impasse by her Foreign

Minister, Antonio Patriota, she burst out and declared that she would then call the meeting herself. Being of the same view, I was happy to see her reaction. Thanks to this, the meeting was held and under her chairpersonship. Not much of importance came out of that encounter. But the tradition had been created. And this would serve us well on the occasion of the next G20 Summit in Mexico, in mid-2012, when the BRICS Leaders met again, and this time took decisions on IMF financing and reform and, more relevant to the topic of this book, on the eventual creation of a common reserve fund by the BRICS.

In Los Cabos, the sticking point was whether it would be appropriate to issue a communiqué or some written statement after the meeting of the BRICS Leaders. The Brazilians were pushing for this to happen because of what we perceived to be the need to make a statement on IMF financing and reform and on the possibility of creating a reserve pooling arrangement, which would later become the CRA. The discussions of a development bank, that would become the NDB, had been launched in the BRICS New Delhi Summit, in March of that year, at a proposal from India.

Indian diplomats felt, however, that it would be "impolite" to issue a separate BRICS statement in Los Cabos, given that the G20 would be issuing its communiqué at the same time. As mentioned, India held the chair of the BRICS in that year, and this created special difficulties. Again, were it not for the determination of the Brazilians, especially of President Dilma Rousseff, no written statement would have come out, and the start of discussions of a reserve pooling arrangement would have probably been postponed to the next BRICS Summit scheduled for South Africa, in early 2013. I will come back to this episode later.

At other times, the difficulty came from Russia. For reasons never clearly explained (Russian matters always seem to involve a dose of mystery and secrecy), Russia would balk at the creation of the NDB and the CRA. We had to spend hours and hours of meetings and negotiations trying to persuade Russian officials that these initiatives made sense. Brazil again often took the lead in these efforts. The fact is that Brazil, from 2009 to 2014, was often the main engine of BRICS financial cooperation. This would change when the political crisis in the country weakened the Rousseff administration substantially as of 2015, leading eventually to her impeachment in 2016.

Common traits of the BRICS

But let us leave these matters aside for a moment and return to the more structural aspects of the BRICS. What do these countries actually have in common that made cooperation among them a rather lasting phenomenon, for 12 years now, since 2008? Even though, as indicated, this cooperation weakened somewhat in more recent years, from 2016/2017 onward.

Part of the answer has already been given in the opening paragraph of this book: the four original members of the group—Brazil, Russia, India, and China—are among the giants of the world, in demographic, territorial, and economic terms. This gives them the *potential* to act independently, with autonomy relatively to the traditional Western powers, the United States and Europe, especially the United States—autonomy with respect to what is sometimes referred to as the North Atlantic axis. This has become increasingly obvious but was not as clear back in 2008 when the BRICS first came together. I stress the word "potential" since, as Brazilian experience shows since 2016, or Russia's in the Yeltsin period back in the 1990s, even a giant can fall back into external dependence and seek alignment with the traditional powers.

Going back, however, to the initial years of the BRICS, what stood out clearly at the time was the contrast between these countries and the vast majority of other emerging market and developing countries (EMDCs) in the different regions of the world. Although small countries can show remarkable resilience and independence—Cuba is a case in point, as well as Iceland, during the 2008–10 financial crisis—ultimately size matters. The great majority of EMDCs did not have the clout to act independently, at least not to the same degree. In the IMF and in the G20, I often witnessed this. The BRICS were actually eager to reach out to other EMDCs to increase our bargaining power. We were rarely successful, however. Exceptions in the IMF were Iran and Argentina, but this depended crucially on the personality of the executive director for these countries.[3] In most cases, what we came up against was a policy of alignment with and even reverence to the United States or the main countries of Europe.

Now, these five large EMDCs had another common trait: all of us were dissatisfied with the way the Bretton Woods institutions were working and their failure to catch up with the changes in the balance of economic and political power in the beginning of the twenty-first century. Brazil, Russia, India, China, and South Africa, as well as other EMDCs, felt strongly that the IMF and the World Bank needed revamping, in terms of the distribution of voting power, the composition of Executive Boards, and the selection of senior management. The distribution of voting power in these institutions bore little relation with economic weights, with EMDCs mostly underrepresented and most of Europe heavily overrepresented. Executive Boards also suffered from an excessive number of Europeans and insufficient presence of developing

3. In the case of Argentina, but not of Iran, this factor varied immensely during my period in the IMF Board, from 2007 to 2015.

countries. The selection of senior management was bound by outdated unwritten rules, especially one that reserved the position of World Bank President to an American national and that of Managing Director of the IMF to a national from a European country. The BRICS joined forces after 2008 to attempt to gradually change this situation.

The capacity of the BRICS to act independently also reflected, it should be noted, their economic and financial positions. None of the BRICS had a high degree of dependence on external capital from the United States or Europe. With the occasional exception of South Africa in some periods, they had strong balance of payments positions coupled with a high level of international reserves. This remains true to this day. We do not require the financial assistance of the IMF and other multilateral financial institutions controlled by the West. On the contrary, as the financial crisis deepened in the United States and Europe in 2008 and 2009, with broad international repercussions, the BRICS were even called upon to become creditors to the IMF, and all of us participated in a concerted effort to increase the institution's financial firepower.[4]

Another point needs to be stressed, lest the wrong impression be given. The approach of the BRICS was never confrontational. It was not anti-United States, although the Americans, always suspicious, may have sometimes understood it that way. We always spoke of, and attempted to practice, cooperation with the countries of the West and with the existing multilateral financial institutions controlled by them. As we will see later in this book, this cooperative approach was clearly reflected in the financial mechanisms—the NDB and the CRA—that the BRICS would subsequently put in place. Thus, our approach was fundamentally different from that of, say, Venezuela during the Chavez and Maduro period or even from that of Argentina during the Kirchner period, not to speak of North Korea or Iran, countries in sharp antagonism with the West.

The BRICS were short on rhetoric and inclined to what could be called a "reformist" approach to international governance. The group sought to be accepted as "responsible" partners in what we hoped could be a common effort to improve and update the international financial architecture. The fact

4. I note in passing that before the 2008 crisis the IMF was critical of the reserve accumulation that ultimately allowed the BRICS to recover from the crisis without requesting IMF support (rather providing support to the Fund). That made the BRICS look suspiciously strong. I address some of these points in a paper published by Boston University. Paulo Nogueira Batista Jr., "The IMF, capital account regulation, and emerging economies," in Kevin P. Gallagher, Stephany Griffith-Jones and José Antonio Ocampo (co-chairs), *Regulating Capital Flows for Long-Run Development*, Pardee Center Task Force Report, University, 2012, pp. 93–102.

that our attempts often fell on deaf ears and were rebutted by Americans and Europeans did not make us give up.

The picture would change for Russia in 2014 with the crisis in Ukraine and the annexation of Crimea. This led to the imposition of widespread sanctions on the country and would have, as I will show, important negative effects on the development of the NDB. However, it can be credibly argued that Russia in this crisis was in effect responding defensively to what they perceived to be a concerted threat, led by the United States. The attempt to gradually attract Ukraine to the European Union and even NATO was seen by the Russians, rightly or not, as a challenge and ultimately a risk to their national security, and they reacted accordingly.

Something similar can be said of China since 2017. The sharp deterioration of US–China relations during the Trump presidency can perhaps be attributed mainly to the stance taken by the US administration. China was on a peaceful rise, as the Chinese say, and did not seem to seek confrontation with the United States. It had nothing to gain from this.

I need not stress that other views can be taken on these matters. Be that as it may, Russia's and China's problems with the West were never entirely taken up by the other BRICS. For Brazil, India, and South Africa there was no point in buying in to these confrontations. And the same holds true for China with respect to Russia, and vice versa. One should not lose sight of the fact that the BRICS formation was never a full-fledged alliance but only a cooperation mechanism for strategic, though limited, purposes.

Chapter 3

CONTINGENT RESERVE ARRANGEMENT—CRA, THE MONETARY FUND OF THE BRICS

I turn now to discuss the financial institutions or mechanisms created by the BRICS, starting with the reserve pooling arrangement, later called the BRICS Contingent Reserve Arrangement (CRA).[1] The origins of the CRA can be traced back to the mid-2000s, to a period preceding the actual establishment of the BRICS in 2008. When I arrived in Washington, DC, in April 2007, to occupy a seat as executive director in the IMF Board, my predecessor in the position, Eduardo Loyo, drew my attention to two issues that pertain to the matter at the hand.

He stressed, first, the enormous difficulty in making any progress at all in terms of IMF reform. This was indeed the situation in the earlier part of 2007. The subsequent financial crisis in the United States and Europe, especially after Lehman collapsed in September 2008, would change the picture and allow us to make progress in this field. But even after 2008, as mentioned above, progress would be limited and always obtained in the teeth of hefty resistance of overrepresented countries, including notably most of Europe.

Second, Loyo told me, it was important to keep an eye on monetary cooperation in East Asia, where 13 countries, led by Japan, China, and South Korea, had been gradually putting into place, since 2000, a reserve pooling arrangement, called the Chiang Mai Initiative. Initially a network of bilateral swap arrangements, Chiang Mai could be seen as an embryonic Asian Monetary Fund, something that was watched with concern by Americans, Europeans, and the Administration of the IMF. Their worry was that this initiative might open the way for a fragmentation of international governance

1. The CRA cannot be called, strictly speaking, an institution, since it possesses no independent international legal personality. Article 19 of the *Treaty for the Establishment of the BRICS Contingent Arrangement*, Fortaleza, Brazil, July 15, 2014 (henceforth referred to as "Treaty"). Throughout the book, I will refer to the financial mechanisms created by the BRICS to take this into account.

and a loss of "centrality" of the IMF, an institution that they tightly controlled. As we know, the Fund was, and remains to this day, essentially a North Atlantic organization. From the point of view of EMDCs, even outside Asia, the establishment of an Asian Monetary Fund was a welcome development as it might exert pressure to move forward with IMF reform and provide a template for similar initiatives in other regions of the world.

The deep international financial crisis of 2008–9, centered on the US and European financial systems, distracted all of us from the issue. Also, G20 negotiations in 2008–10 held up the expectation that IMF reform might after all make substantial progress. I cannot dwell on these matters in this book. Suffice to say that, despite American and European commitments at the highest possible level, that is, at the Leaders' level in the G20, IMF reform moved forward very slowly. A sort of betrayal had happened. The BRICS had been led to cooperate with the Western powers in overcoming their financial crisis. We had provided substantial financial resources to the IMF—by lending and not by acquiring quotas and voting power—but had been subsequently disappointed in our expectations of real change in the IMF. Something similar can be said of the World Bank. In the IMF, China, Brazil, and India did obtain significant quota and voting power increases, but actual implementation of the reform proved excruciatingly slow and would come into force only as late as January/February 2016. Moreover, the actual shift of voting power to EMDCs as a whole was modest, leaving the balance of power within the institution largely untouched. Russia and South Africa, for instance, even lost voting power. Executive Board composition underwent mostly cosmetic changes, due to European resistance. The unwritten rule reserving the post of managing director to a national of a European country remained. Forward-looking elements of IMF reform—a further review of the quota formula, as well as of quotas and votes, steps initially foreseen for 2013 and 2014, respectively—were never implemented.[2]

By 2010, or even earlier, it was crystal clear that we had to increase the pressure on the West if we hoped to achieve anything at all. Since 2008, the BRICS were meeting regularly, including at the level of finance minister and Central Bank governors. Could the BRICS take up the issue of monetary cooperation, I asked myself, and send a message to the IMF that we were willing to go our own way in response to the resistance to reform in Washington? The Brazilian Finance Minister Guido Mantega often took the lead in these

2. I discuss these matters at length in a book published in Brazil at the end of 2019. Paulo Nogueira Batista Jr., *O Brasil não cabe no quintal de ninguém: bastidores da vida de um economista brasileiro no FMI e nos BRICS e outros textos sobre nacionalismo e nosso complexo de vira-lata*, São Paulo, LeYa, 2019, pp. 33–231.

discussions. As early as October 2008, at the meeting of the International Monetary and Financial Committee (IMFC) of the IMF, he stated that in light of the limitations of the IMF and other existing international financial mechanisms, emerging market and developing countries "would have to rely on the protection provided by their own international reserves or on regional reserve pooling arrangements."[3]

My initial approach to the matter was extremely complicated and would prove unworkable. I proposed to minister Mantega that we contemplate creating other regional financial or reserve pooling arrangements, similar to the Chiang Mai Initiative, centered on Brazil, Russia, India, and South Africa. Something along these lines already existed at the time, initiated by Russia and India with neighboring countries. The idea was to establish similar schemes around Brazil and South Africa with their respective neighbors and then link the five reserve pooling arrangements in a financial network of mutual balance of payments support. Mantega asked me to present this proposal in BRICS ministerial and other meetings, and I did so, in more detail when the BRICS finance ministers and Central Bank governors met in Busan, South Korea, in June 2010, on the sidelines of a G20 ministerial meeting. Brazil held the presidency of the BRICS process in that year and a few months before that, in the second Annual Summit in Brasília, in April, we had managed to include in the joint statement of the Leaders a sentence asking finance ministers and Central Bank governors to look into regional monetary arrangements and discuss modalities of cooperation between our countries in this area.[4] But not much happened in practice until 2012.

The proposal of interlinking five regional reserve pooling arrangements was ambitious and politically attractive but involved the participation of an excessively large number of countries. In Latin America and the Caribbean, for instance, we were far from the level of coordination and mutual understanding that had led East Asian countries to come together in the Chiang Mai Initiative, a trend that harked back to their 2007 crisis and the many mistakes made by the IMF at the time, prompting these countries to design alternative forms of support in emergencies. Moreover, the Central Bank of Brazil was strongly opposed, perhaps rightly so, to committing Brazilian international reserves, even in limited amounts, to providing balance-of-payment support to our neighbors, some of them conducting highly problematic economic policies. Similar issues might arise in other regions.

3. Guido Mantega, *Statement to the 18th Meeting of the IMFC*, Washington, DC, October 2008, p. 4.
4. *Second BRIC Summit of Heads of State and Government—Joint Statement*, Brasília, April 15, 2010, paragraph 12.

Brazil and China take the lead

In early 2012, however, Minister Guido Mantega came up with a simpler proposal that had arisen in conversations with the Chinese Central Bank governor, Zhou Xiaochuan. This would be to create a transregional reserve pooling arrangement involving, at least initially, only the five BRICS countries. Brazilian President Dilma Rousseff, Mantega told me, was strongly supportive of the proposal, and he asked me to flesh out an initial version. I had no difficulty in doing so, with support of some members of my team in the Brazilian office in the IMF. We took as inspiration not only the Chiang Mai Initiative but the IMF itself—a reserve pooling arrangement in its own right—as well as bilateral swap agreements between Central Banks.

The international reserves of the five countries taken together were as high as US$ 4.5 trillion at the time, with China accounting for around 70 percent of the total, an amount more than sufficient to support the initiative that was being proposed. As outlined by us, the reserve fund could be set in motion by any country facing balance of payments pressures and external financing difficulties. The fund could be of a virtual nature, we anticipated, in the sense that reserves would remain with the Central Banks to be made available as needs arose, avoiding the creation of a new bureaucracy. Since the position of the five countries was mostly solid (with the occasional exception of South Africa in certain periods), there was no expectation that the mechanism would often be put to actual use, but its existence could by itself provide a strengthening of confidence and deepen BRICS cooperation.

When could we launch the process? The earliest opportunity would be the already mentioned BRICS Leaders' meeting on the sidelines of the G20 Summit, scheduled for Los Cabos, Mexico, in June 2012. Brazil would prepare the documents for the decision, supported by China. The Chinese, sensing perhaps that resistance might be greater if they were the ones to take the lead, asked the Brazilians to come forward. Of course, what led the Chinese to make this proposal to the Brazilian side was the role that we had played in previous discussions of the topic in the BRICS context, as indicated before.

Things did not proceed smoothly, however. I arrived early in Los Cabos with the task of putting together with the other four countries a document outlining a possible reserve fund to be taken for the consideration of the BRICS Leaders. Discussions were difficult, with Russian officials in particular showing considerable reticence. I could not count on the Brazilian Central Bank, ever suspicious of anything involving a commitment of international reserves of which they were the depository. The governor of the Central Bank, Alexandre Tombini, was wary of any such proposal, even in cooperation with countries such as China, Russia, and India, all of them like Brazil possessing high international reserves, especially China. Were it not for the determination of President Dilma Rousseff, I doubt that his resistance would have been overcome.[5]

Help from the Chinese side allowed us to move forward. We eventually managed to reach a consensus on a draft of a short announcement on reserve pooling and currency swap arrangements that could be accepted by the Leaders. The draft announcement noted that the size and spillover effects of recent economic and financial crises had brought to the forefront the importance of strengthening safety nets beyond the financial support of the International Monetary Fund and countries' international reserves. In order to forestall liquidity pressures, provide mutual support, and further strengthen financial stability, the Leaders would agree, we suggested, to explore together the possibility of setting up a multilateral currency swap arrangement by way of creating a reserve pool to which each of our countries would pledge to contribute up to a preestablished amount. These resources could be drawn upon in case one of our countries should require support. This initiative, together with bilateral currency swaps in national currencies, could contribute to strengthen the global financial safety net and was to be viewed as a complement to the existing international arrangements. The Leaders, it was proposed, would ask their finance ministers and Central Bank governors to work on the implementation of these proposals, in compatibility with internal legal procedures, and report back to them by March 2013.[6]

This was the essence of the document agreed by officials of the five countries in the days preceding the Leaders' meeting. I kept Minister Mantega aware of the steps taken in Los Cabos and he, in turn, informed President Dilma Rousseff.

As indicated above, in March 2012, in their annual Summit, held in New Delhi in India, the BRICS Leaders had directed their finance ministers to examine the feasibility of setting up a new development bank. In the run-up

---

5. For non-Brazilian readers, it may be useful to point out that although the Brazilian Central Bank did not possess full legal independence and the members of its Board did not have fixed mandates, it enjoyed a good deal of autonomy in practice. Thus, its resistance to the initiative was a barrier of considerable importance. Even a strong-willed and determined president, as Dilma Rousseff certainly was, could not simply force the Central Bank to fall into line. Though she could be counted upon to make things ultimately move forward, this did not free me from having to struggle repeatedly with obstacles raised by Central Bank officials, as I will explain subsequently.
6. "BRICS Leaders' Announcement on Reserve Pooling and Currency Swap Arrangements," draft, Los Cabos, June 18, 2012, available at https://www.nogueirabatista.com.br/category/documentos/brics/cra/.

to the meeting in Los Cabos, our goal was to obtain from the Leaders a similar go-ahead for the monetary fund or reserve pooling arrangement, as indicated in the draft announcement. For this to work, however, we had to persuade everyone that the meeting in Los Cabos, although presented as "informal", would produce some sort of communiqué or written statement by the Leaders, something that had not happened before. In Cannes, no communiqué had been issued.

I was confident that this would be possible but encountered unexpected difficulties from the Indian side. India presided over the BRICS process in 2012, as mentioned earlier, and thus chaired all the meetings. At the last minute, only a few days before the Leaders were scheduled to meet, the Indian Sherpa, Montek Singh Ahluwalia, a high-ranking diplomatic official, objected that it would be impolite and inconvenient to issue a separate statement, undermining, he claimed, the G20 communiqué to be issued in Los Cabos. The other Indian officials explained to me that, given the political importance of the Sherpa, who was close to Prime Minister Manmohan Singh, this would create serious difficulties.

As the meeting started, in the morning of June 18, President Dilma Rousseff, having arrived the previous evening in Los Cabos, was unfortunately unaware of this last-minute obstacle. Minister Mantega had not managed to get the message to her and she went into the meeting fully confident that everything had been arranged beforehand.

I am dwelling on this episode at some length because I believe it is illustrative of how international negotiations play out in the real world. I ask the reader to picture the situation. We find ourselves in a rather small room in a hotel in Los Cabos. The five Leaders are there, Rousseff, Putin, Singh, Hu Jintao, and Zuma, each of them accompanied by five or six officials. About 25 to 30 people, crowded in a hotel office. The meeting, chaired by the Indian Prime Minister Singh, starts, and covers the world economy, the eurozone crisis, IMF reform, and other matters. The reserve pooling arrangement, however—arguably one of the main, if not the main, topics—is not put on the table by Prime Minister Singh, reflecting the reluctance of the Indian Sherpa. As the meeting closes without a discussion of the reserve fund, President Dilma explodes in frustration and complains harshly with Minister Mantega and the rest of the Brazilian delegation. An awkward situation. Looking across the small, crowded room, one could notice that Putin, Singh, Hu Jintao, and Zuma, already standing, were observing the Brazilian president's outburst with some perplexity, although they could of course not understand what she was saying. Immediately after her outburst, Dilma Rousseff walked to the Chinese side to speak to Hu Jintao. I accompanied her. So, there we stood, Hu Jintao and two Chinese officials, Dilma and me, plus interpreters, with the Brazilian president expressing her disappointment at the lack of progress on the reserve fund. The Chinese president agreed with everything she said and promised to do his best to advance the proposal. Meanwhile, Brazilian diplomats, impressed by their president's commitment to the idea, went to the Indian side to express our disagreement with the behavior of the chair.

We left the meeting in frustration. Work on the reserve fund, we thought, had probably been set back by eight or nine months to the next BRICS Summit, scheduled for South Africa in the beginning of 2013. To our surprise, however, the Indian chair did something highly unusual. After the meeting, India issued a "media note" (a language trick probably to assuage the Indian Sherpa's concerns) informing that the BRICS Leaders had discussed swap arrangements among national currencies as well as reserve pooling. They had agreed, the media note stated, to ask their finance ministers and Central Bank governors to work on this important issue, in a manner compatible with internal legal frameworks, reporting back to the Leaders at the 2013 BRICS Summit.[7] This had not happened at all but was the go-ahead we needed. Dilma Rousseff's explosion had worked in the end. A somewhat unconventional, but nevertheless effective manner of advancing an international negotiation.

Work on the CRA begins

A working group was then set up, chaired by Brazil. The Brazilians had proposed sharing the coordination with China. In the case of the development bank, a working group composed of Finance Ministry officials had been established, cochaired by India and South Africa. But the Chinese preferred to take a back seat, probably for the reasons indicated above. The reserve fund working group came to be composed mainly of Central Bank officials, only Brazil and South Africa were also represented by Finance Ministry officials. The chairman was Fernando Pimentel, a young Brazilian diplomat seconded to the Finance Ministry at the time, who would become an effective coordinator. Unfortunately, I was the only IMF executive director participating in the group—had my BRICS colleagues in the Board also been included, work would have proceeded much more efficiently, given their excellent technical preparation and political clarity, especially of the Russian chair, led by Aleksei Mozhin, and of the Indian chair, led at the time by Arvind Virmani and subsequently Rakesh Mohan.

Although natural in a sense, the composition of the working group, later transformed into a negotiating group, would prove harmful. With the

7. "Media note on the informal meeting of BRICS Leaders ahead of the G20 Summit in Los Cabos," Los Cabos, Mexico, June 18, 2012.

exception of the Chinese, and notably of their former IMF executive director, He Jianxiong, and also of a few Indian participants, Central Bank officials took a rather narrow and cautious view of the matter, and this was true especially of Brazilian Central Bank officials, who later became a stumbling block in the process.

In view of the reluctance of the Brazilian Central Bank that initially tried simply to stay away from the initiative, hoping perhaps that it would die away, the Brazilian executive director's office in the IMF became, in practice, the secretariat for the working group and subsequently for the negotiations. The Brazilian Finance Ministry did not possess the human resources and technical knowledge to carry out the task, and the few persons involved, mostly diplomats on loan to the Ministry, were also burdened at the same time with the negotiations that would lead to the creation of the NDB. So my office in the IMF, with limited support from Brasília, carried out the work of preparing the documents for the working group and the negotiations, the simulations of different scenarios, and the evolving drafts of the agreement for the creation of the reserve fund, early on named the Contingent Reserve Arrangement (CRA), as well as the formulation of Brazil's negotiating positions. I could only play this role because of my ties and access to the Brazilian Minister of Finance Guido Mantega, who was, in turn, close to President Dilma Rousseff. Also important were my informal exchanges and understandings with the Chinese, who had considerable experience and knowledge of the topic, given China's role in the Chiang Mai Initiative.[8]

It should also be noted in passing that work in the preparation and negotiation of what would become the CRA was entirely compatible with the role of executive director in the IMF. Executive directors in the Fund are allowed to provide technical assistance to the countries they represent in the institution, and can even charge for this, which I did not. Moreover, as the BRICS meetings on the development bank and the reserve fund often occurred in the same venues, on the sidelines of G20 or IMF meetings, I also participated on several occasions in meetings related to the creation of the development bank—never wishing or imagining that I would eventually become one of the founding members of the institution.

Work proceeded in the second half of 2012 and early 2013, but the BRICS had yet to take the actual decision to create the CRA and the NDB, as our Russian colleagues repeatedly stressed in the working group meetings. The matter would have to be settled in BRICS Leaders' Summit, in Durban, South Africa, in March 2013. We had no guarantee that this would indeed happen, mostly because of Russia's reluctance. Again, this reluctance was something of a

8. Revised and renamed Chiang Mai Initiative Multilateralization (CMIM) in 2009.

mystery. The Russian officials I was closer to in the IMF conveyed to me the view that it came mostly from the Finance Ministry and the Central Bank, and that President Putin, strongly supportive of the BRICS process, was bound to agree to move forward when the matter came to his level. So, we had reason to hope.

As it turned out, the Russian Finance Minister Anton Siluanov surprised us in Durban, in the meeting of finance ministers and Central Bank governors one day ahead of the BRICS Summit itself, by suddenly agreeing to create the CRA but, unfortunately, continuing to object to the creation of the NDB. No plausible reasons were given, but the difficulty was there. In the event, President Zuma's desire to have "deliverables" at the Summit presided by him, as well as his strong wish to see the creation of our development bank, led the South Africans to force the issue and to make a last minute inclusion to the Leaders' communiqué indicating their decision to create both the NDB and the CRA. President Putin seemed unmoved by this, as predicted by my Russian IMF colleagues, but Minister Siluanov excitedly complained about the maneuver, behind the scenes, with his South African colleague, Finance Minister Pravin Gordhan. Anyway, the matter stuck. And, again without clear explanations, but possibly due to geopolitical considerations arising from the deepening crisis in Ukraine, the Russian economic authorities fell subsequently in line and contributed to the negotiations of the NDB and the CRA.

Main issues involved in the negotiation of the CRA

Before coming to the NDB, let us examine in some detail the issues involved in the negotiation of the CRA. First and foremost came the size of the reserve pool. China, having as it did immense international reserves, proposed a large amount, up to US$ 240 billion. The other countries were much more modest. Russia and India spoke initially of only US$ 50 billion. South Africa, the only BRICS country with small reserves, was not willing or capable of contributing any large amount. Brazil was hampered by our Central Bank's opposition to the initiative, but the finance minister fully realized that anything much below US$ 100 billion would not make any impact at all.

An exceptionally large amount would make China dominate entirely the CRA. So, the challenge was to reconcile our desire to produce an impact and create something relevant, with the concern of avoiding Chinese dominance. The Chinese were relatively flexible in this respect, making our life easier. With the help of members of my team in Washington,[9] I started experimenting with

9. Especially Ivan de Oliveira Lima, Fabio Najjarian Batista, and, in the initial stages, also Luis Mansur. All three were Central Bank officials, hired by or seconded to the Brazilian executive director's office in the IMF.

different formulas for the distribution of country contributions, access limits, and voting power in the CRA. After exploring a great deal of approaches and discussing, sometimes at interminable length, with officials from the five countries, we eventually settled on the following solution.

To cut a complicated discussion short, I will stick to the essentials. It was decided that China would commit US$ 41 billion; Brazil, India, and Russia, US$ 18 billion each; and South Africa US$ 5 billion, totaling US$ 100 billion initially.[10] Thus, China would not have a simple majority of the contributions. We agreed that most decisions would be taken by consensus but that the crucial decisions on requests for support or renewal of support would depend on a simple majority of votes, weighed mostly by the size of contributions of each country. Requiring consensus in the sense of unanimity for these decisions would of course give veto power to all five countries, something definitely to be avoided. I therefore resisted all attempts by some Central Bank officials, notably the Russians and again the Brazilians, to establish consensus as an overall rule in the CRA. In this respect, China helped again by arguing that their substantially larger contribution had to be reflected in some way in the decision-making rules of the CRA. On the other hand, to further reduce Chinese dominance, we introduced basic votes, as in the IMF, with 5 percent of voting power being distributed equally among the five countries.[11] As a result, voting power was defined as follows: China 39.95 percent of votes; Brazil, Russia, and India, 18.1 percent each; and South Africa, 5.75 percent.[12] Thus, even China alone could not normally exercise any veto over decisions to provide or renew support.[13]

The above-mentioned contributions to the CRA would not be disbursed into a common fund but remain with the Central Banks of the participating countries.[14] In other words, the CRA would be a virtual and not an actual reserve pooling arrangement—in this respect equal to Chiang Mai (also a

---

10. Article 2 (a) of the Treaty.
11. Article 3 (e) of the Treaty.
12. For a discussion of these matters, see Jonnas Esmeraldo Marques de Vasconcelos, *BRICS: Agenda regulatória*, 2018. Tese (Doutorado)—Faculdade de Direito da Universidade de São Paulo, São Paulo, 2018, pp. 156–59, https://bdpi.usp.br/item/002910177.
13. "Normally" because the picture would change in the unlikely event that two countries (or more) should need support at the same time. In this case, China would hold a simple majority of the providing countries and would be able to veto any of these requests. To avoid or mitigate even this remote possibility, we tried to have a much higher proportion of basic votes, but the Chinese resisted strenuously and in the end we settled for basic votes at 5 percent of total voting power.
14. Article 2 (b) of the Treaty.

virtual arrangement) and different from the IMF (an actual reserve pooling arrangement). Disbursements would only be made if one of the participating countries should need support and decide to draw on the CRA. Support would be provided through currency swaps between the Central Banks of the requesting country and those of the providing countries. These swaps would involve an exchange of the currency of the requesting country for US dollars provided by the Central Banks of the providing countries in proportion to their share of the reserve fund.[15]

Early on in the negotiations, at the suggestion of China, we agreed that the CRA would foresee two types of support: (a) a liquidity instrument to respond to short-term balance of payments pressures; and (b) a precautionary instrument committing to provide support in light of potential pressures.[16] This distinction was taken from features of the Chiang Mai Initiative, as well as from the IMF, where disbursing facilities coexist with precautionary facilities.

It was also agreed that governance of the CRA would be constituted by a Council of CRA Governors (the "Governing Council") and a Standing Committee. The Governing Council would be comprised of one governor and one alternate for each country, with governors necessarily being a finance minister, a Central Bank governor, or a person holding an equivalent post. The Governing Council would take decisions by consensus and be responsible for high-level and strategic decisions.[17] The Standing Committee would be in charge of executive-level and operational decisions and be comprised of one director and one alternate director per country appointed from Central Bank officials unless decided otherwise by a country.[18] During the negotiations, the Central Banks tried to reserve the positions of CRA governors and especially of members of the Standing Committee exclusively for the Central Bank officials, but I managed to rebuff the idea, not without difficulty. After the Treaty entered into force, however, the main positions were held by Central Bank governors and officials anyway, something that for reasons already mentioned would prove harmful to the development of the CRA.

A number of other sticking points arose in the negotiations. How much could each country draw or request as precautionary support? What conditions would it have to fulfill to request support? Could a country refuse to participate in support of another, that is, invoke some sort of opt-out clause? Could resources disbursed continue to be counted as international reserves, that is,

15. Articles 7, 8, and 15 (a) of the Treaty.
16. Article 4 of the Treaty.
17. Article 3 (b) of the Treaty.
18. Article 3 (c) of the Treaty.

could the CRA ensure so-called encashability of disbursed resources, as in the IMF?

Maximum access to the CRA would be determined by individual contributions times a multiplier.[19] Possessing immense reserves, China had of course no need or intention of requesting support from the CRA and thus settled for a multiplier of 0.5, a mere formality. Brazil, Russia, and India settled for a multiplier of 1, meaning that each of them could draw a maximum of US$ 18 billion. South Africa, the weakest country of the group in terms of balance of payments and international reserves, obtained a multiplier of 2, meaning that it could draw a maximum of US$ 10 billion. If, for example, South Africa were to draw the maximum available amount, China would have to come forward with US$ 4.3 billion and Brazil, Russia, and India with US$ 1.9 billion each. Given the size of their international reserves, these were not inordinately large amounts, especially for short-term swap agreements,[20] but the Brazilian Central Bank, for instance, was worried at the prospect of providing reserves to South Africa.[21] Strangely enough, some South African Central Bank officials, naively oblivious of this, often joined forces with Brazilian central bankers and others in making the CRA less flexible in terms of disbursement than it could be.

19. Article 5 (a) of the Treaty.
20. Maturities for CRA operations were limited to a maximum of one year, with a maximum of three renewals, depending on whether disbursements were linked to the IMF and on whether support was provided through the liquidity or the precautionary instrument. Article 12 of the Treaty. See also Marques de Vasconcelos, *BRICS: Agenda regulatória*, p. 164. The Treaty also established that interest rates to be paid would be based on an internationally accepted benchmark plus a spread. In the case of the precautionary instrument, the amount committed but not drawn would be subject, as usual, to a commitment fee. Article 11 of the Treaty. The actual values for spreads and commitment fees, as well as other financial features of the CRA, were left to be specified in a separate agreement between the Central Banks.
21. Even if Brazil, Russia, or India were to draw the maximum available amounts, the required effort from the other countries was perfectly manageable. For instance, if India were to ask for the full amount, China would have to supply US$ 9 billion, Brazil and Russia US$ 3.9 billion each, and South Africa US$ 1.1 billion. Given its lower level of reserves, South Africa might balk at the prospect of providing resources. It could, however, invoke the opt-out clause, to be explained below. Only in South Africa's case would the required disbursement exceed 2 percent of the country's international reserves at the time of the negotiations. These figures come from simulations prepared by my office in the IMF and presented at a Working Group meeting. *BRICS CRA*, Working Group Meeting, in Washington, DC, October 8, 2013, tables 9, 10 and 11, available at https://www.nogueirabatista.com.br/category/documentos/brics/cra/.

To what extent should the CRA be linked to the IMF?

The issue was then to establish the conditions that a requesting country would have to fulfill to request support. Automatic drawing of the full amounts allotted to each country (total use of access limits) was never contemplated by anyone. The BRICS countries did not in effect have any capacity to carry out surveillance or, needless to say, impose any sort of conditionality on a requesting country. Imposition of conditionality would be politically unthinkable anyway. Thus, the natural solution would be to piggyback on the IMF.

It could thus be said that, beyond the unlinked portion, it was ultimately a matter of "our money with IMF conditionality," another reason to say that the BRICS had no intention of antagonizing with the IMF. China as the main providing country was inclined to strongly stress the IMF link. At the start of the negotiations, it went so far as to suggest that the free portion be kept at zero, meaning that the CRA would be fully linked to the IMF. This made no sense. However, the Chinese negotiators, taking instructions from Governor Zhou of the Central Bank, to whom Minister Mantega spoke about this, soon agreed to allow 10 percent of maximum access on a more or less automatic manner, without IMF presence or conditionality, the level at which Chiang Mai had originally started. To draw beyond that a country would have to have an agreement with the IMF in place.

A 10 percent threshold was still too low, and the Brazilians, meaning Finance Ministry officials and the Brazilians in the IMF, as well as others, pushed from the beginning for a higher free portion. At one point, however, Brazilian Central Bank officials came back to the rather strange proposal of simply eliminating the free portion and thus having 100 percent link with the IMF. This defeated the whole purpose of the exercise. Why create a monetary fund of the BRICS if it were to be fully linked to the IMF? CRA resources, exclusively provided by BRICS countries, would be completely tied up to the decision-making process of the IMF, a process that these countries severely criticized. With help from Finance Ministry officials, I managed to kick this proposal out of court but at some cost in terms of weakening the Brazilian negotiating position and of harming my relations with the Central Bank. Strange as this may seem, at a late stage of the negotiations, when China—with reserves more than eight times higher than Brazil—had already agreed to a 20 percent free portion, the Brazilian Central Bank was still trying to fix it at only 10 percent of total access.

I would like to impress upon the reader how difficult it was to solve these matters, even with only five countries around the table (or six, taking into account that the Brazilian Central Bank, to my amazement, often behaved as a "sixth BRICS"). Keeping Brazilian Central Bank officials more or less in line was next to impossible.[22] I would, now and then, lose my temper with some of them, making for unpleasant situations. Often, Central Bank *esprit de corps* or *camaraderie* made the proposals coming from these Brazilian officials resonate more or less with other central bankers, even when they were technically unsound or made the arrangement less flexible or less effective. The level of the participating officials was not always high, with a number of notable exceptions such as most of the Chinese, especially He Jianxiong, and the chief Indian negotiator, Urjit Patel, who later became the head of the Reserve Bank of India, as well as some other Indian central bankers. The Brazilian chair, Fernando Pimentel, began with little understanding of the matter but did his best and was an able go-between and fast learner. The driving force during the negotiations was the Brazilian office in the IMF, resulting in enormous sacrifices for my team and myself, since we took care of the CRA negotiations in addition to all our heavy obligations to the IMF's Executive Board agenda.[23]

Extracting from the Chinese a higher free portion was quite a challenge. China wanted to keep it low until the CRA could manage to create its own surveillance unit. Chiang Mai had started with a low free portion, at 10 percent of total access, and increased it gradually as it established its surveillance unit in Singapore, named the ASEAN +3 Macroeconomic Research Office (AMRO). At the time of our negotiations, the free portion in Chiang Mai

22. The problem increased over time as the political position of Finance Minister Guido Mantega weakened during 2014, leading to his replacement at the end of that year. The Central Bank governor, Alexandre Tombini, who was, as indicated, wary of the CRA, would remain in office for the remainder of the Dilma Rousseff Administration until 2016.

23. This would not have been possible at all, I observe in passing, were it not for the considerable strengthening of the Brazilian chair in the IMF after 2008, thanks chiefly to the support of the Brazilian government, from the Minister of Finance at the political level, and from the Foreign Ministry and the Central Bank in terms of provisions of human resources on secondment. Particularly important was the role of Eduardo Saboia and Felipe Santarosa from the Foreign Ministry, as well as that of the already mentioned officials from the Central Bank of Brazil. Thus, the Central Bank helped and hindered me at the same time. Also instrumental, I should say critical, to my backup, while I was away from Washington in BRICS meetings around the world, was the change in the structure of the Brazilian chair with the departure of Colombia and the possibility I thereby acquired of nominating the experienced Hector Torres, from Argentina, as alternate executive director in our chair. Officials from Trinidad and Tobago, Haiti, and Nicaragua also assisted considerably in our work in the IMF Board. Toward the end of my period in the IMF, the entry of Pedro Fachada, also from the Central Bank of Brazil, as alternate executive director meant a further valuable addition to the Brazilian chair. The strengthening of the Brazilian position in the IMF Board in the 2008–15 period is described at length in the book I published at the end of 2019. Nogueira Batista Jr., *O Brasil não cabe no quintal de ninguém*, pp. 97–118.

stood at 30 percent. Only in the very last meeting of the negotiating group before the Fortaleza Summit, in June 2014, did I manage to have the Chinese finally agree that the CRA would also have a 30 percent free portion, unlinked to the IMF, despite the fact that a surveillance unit would not be established immediately. Any amount above this limit would require the existence of an arrangement with the IMF, a precondition defined quite strictly as the existence of an on-track arrangement between the country and the IMF, involving financing based on conditionality, and compliance of the country with the terms and conditions of the arrangement.[24]

The IMF link was the main precondition for access to the CRA beyond the 30 percent threshold. But a rather long list of other preconditions was established, also for the free portion, including submission of all required economic and financial data, ensuring that obligations under the CRA would rank at least *pari passu* with all other foreign debts, no arrears with the public financial institutions of the providing countries and with the NDB or other multilateral and regional financial institutions, as well as compliance with surveillance and provision of information obligations under Article IV and Article VIII of the Articles of Agreement of the IMF.[25]

Other sticking points in the negotiations

A permanent secretariat for the CRA or a surveillance unit similar to AMRO was foreseen in the Treaty,[26] to be created in due course. Six years after the CRA Treaty was signed in July 2014, however, this has not yet happened, due to disagreements between the countries as to where to locate it. China offered Shanghai and spoke of hosting the CRA surveillance unit in the same building as the NDB. My own view at the time of the negotiations and shortly thereafter was that this would be an inconvenient proposal, as it would transform Shanghai, so to speak, into the new Washington, DC for the BRICS, headquartering the development bank and the reserve fund. Chinese dominance of the financing mechanisms created by the BRICS would become excessive, given that the choice of location has an important practical effect in molding institutions, as clearly shown by several decades of experience with international organizations. Early 2015, I persuaded the Brazilian government to come forward with Rio de Janeiro as an alternative. India later also claimed an interest in hosting the surveillance unit. The fact that no decision

24. Article 5 (d, ii) of the Treaty.
25. Article 14 of the Treaty.
26. Article 3 (b, ix) of the Treaty.

has been taken to this day is an indication of the loss of momentum of the BRICS process in recent years.

But let us return to the last stage of the negotiations in the first half of 2014. Brazilian Central Bank officials were quite unhappy, even more than the Chinese, as mentioned, about the relatively high size of the free portion, and sought to compensate for this by creating other difficulties. Thanks to their insistence, the CRA Treaty would contain an excessively generous opt-out clause. I tried as best I could to introduce language to avoid or at least mitigate this problem, but the result was not entirely satisfactory. As Urjit Patel noted during the negotiation, the way Brazilian central bankers wanted to formulate the provision, proposing that countries be free to stay away from a request for support, was inconsistent, strictly speaking, with the principles of a reserve pooling arrangement. As eventually formulated in the Treaty, countries were allowed to opt out from participating in the provision of support, provided this was justified by their balance of payments and reserve position or by an event of *force majeure*, such as a war or a natural disaster. The country opting out could simply inform the others by providing the necessary information.[27] A rather weak compromise solution.

Another way of downplaying the role of the CRA was to create obstacles to the admittance of new countries and to increases in the size of the arrangement beyond the initial US$ 100 billion. My intention was to leave these possibilities open as they would make the BRICS reserve pool gradually more relevant. Others, however, feared that this could lead to excessive commitments and the entry of weak countries, a possible threat to the international reserves of the BRICS countries. In the end, it was agreed that decisions to increase the size of the CRA and admit new participants would require a consensus at the level of the Board of Governors being therefore subject to the veto of any of the members. As these decisions mean amendments to the Treaty, they also require another process of ratification in the Parliaments of the participating countries.[28]

Finally, encashability of resources supplied by any country was guaranteed by allowing it to request prepayment of outstanding claims (so-called encashment) provided this was justified by its balance of payments and reserve position or by an event of *force majeure*, such as a war or a natural disaster—the same language used in the opt-out clause. The other providing countries

---

27. Article 15 (c) of the Treaty. This weakness of the CRA was noticed by a careful researcher of the BRICS process. Marquesde Vasconcelos, *BRICS: Agenda regulatória*, p. 169.
28. With the exception of China and India, where approval of the Treaty and any amendments do not depend on Parliament.

would then step in to supply the required resources in proportion to their commitments to the CRA. However, to apply this clause the country asking for encashment not only had the obligation of providing the necessary information to justify the request but also needed to obtain the approval of the other providing parties.[29] A subtle but important difference in comparison to the opt-out clause, where no such approval was foreseen.

Despite all these disagreements among the participants, the negotiations were successful in the end and we managed to have the Treaty signed in Fortaleza, at the Brazilian Summit, in July 2014. On the same occasion, the Articles of Agreement of the NDB were also signed.

Ratification, acceptance, or approval of these two documents by Parliaments or other State bodies[30] proceeded quickly, although not without considerable efforts of explanation, in which I participated in Brasília. One year later, the process had been completed in the five countries. When the BRICS Leaders met again in Ufa, Russia, in July 2015, they could announce that the CRA and the NDB were ready to commence. By that time, I had left the IMF and was on my way to Shanghai to take up the position of vice president of the NDB.

Developments after the Fortaleza and Ufa Summits

A final quick word is warranted on the development of the CRA after the signing of the Treaty and its ratification or approval. The word can be quick because not much of great relevance occurred, unfortunately.

In describing the outcomes of the negotiation, I have already hinted at some of the problems that would be felt in the following years. Having fallen into the hands exclusively of Central Bank officials, something I did my best to avoid, unsuccessfully in the end, the CRA moved slowly after the Fortaleza and Ufa BRICS Leaders' Summits. Again, the participation and even leadership of Central Bank officials is warranted, given the nature of the initiative. However, the absence of representatives from other sectors of the governments in the CRA's Standing Committee, notably Finance Ministry officials, was unfortunate. I note, in passing, that finance ministers and their subordinates play a key role in other monetary funds, in the Chiang Mai Initiative, for instance, and also in the IMF.[31]

---

29. Article 15 (d) of the Treaty.
30. By the State Council in China and by the Cabinet of Union Government in India.
31. In the IMF, countries are represented in the Board of Governors, more often than not, by their finance ministers or the equivalent. Executive directors or alternate executive directors in the IMF Board are often high-ranking officials from the Finance Ministries. In Chiang Mai, political and strategic decisions are taken in regular meetings of the finance ministers and Central Bank governors of the member countries.

In the event, nothing was done to expand the CRA during its first five years of existence. The total amount of commitments remains at US$ 100 billion, making the CRA small when compared to other reserve pooling arrangements.[32] My initial expectation was that over time, with the development of the operational mechanisms of the CRA and the detailed specification of guarantees for the providing parties, in the Treaty itself and in subsequent understandings among the participating Central Banks, confidence and mutual trust would increase, allowing a gradual expansion of commitments by the BRICS. As things stand, the maximum amount that can be supplied under the CRA remains limited. Only for South Africa are they significant. Furthermore, given that access above the 30 percent threshold is linked to the existence of an arrangement with the IMF, it is unlikely that any of the BRICS would draw above that limit. And the free portion, delinked from the IMF, provides small amounts, even for South Africa.[33]

The same can be said of membership expansion, another way of increasing the size of the arrangement and its international importance. The CRA remains a five-country arrangement to this day and, in so far as I know, no steps have been taken to expand membership. Reluctance with respect to new members was already indicated, by the way, in the choice of the arrangement's name—BRICS CRA, in contrast with the development bank, named deliberately New Development Bank and not BRICS Development Bank.

Toward the end of my period as executive director in the IMF, authorized by Minister Mantega, I had initiated preliminary understandings with most

---

32. Total commitments under the CMIM, for example, were expanded to US$ 240 billion in 2014. Asian Development Bank, *Chiang Mai Initiative [Multilateralization]*, Asia Regional Integration Center: Tracking Asian Integration, https://aric.adb.org/initiative/chiang-mai-initiative.

33. I was, of course, fully aware of these limitations at the time of the negotiations and was actually at pains to stress them in order to assuage the concerns of some of the Central Banks, especially that of Brazil. See, for example, *BRICS CRA*, Working Group Meeting, Washington, DC, October 8, 2013; and, also, *Contingent Reserve Arrangement (CRA)—Impacto para o Brasil*, Office of the Executive Director—Paulo Nogueira Batista Jr., OEDBR, International Monetary Fund, Washington, DC, October 20, 2013. Both documents are available at https://www.nogueirabatista.com.br/category/documentos/brics/cra. For instance, the maximum delinked drawing would provide US$ 3 billion for South Africa, the equivalent of 6.2 percent of its international reserves in June 2013; full access would provide US$ 10 billion, equivalent to 21 percent of the country's reserves at the time. For India, the maximum delinked drawing and full access would bring US$ 5.4 billion and US$ 18 billion, respectively, only 1.8 percent and 6.3 percent of its reserves at the time. For Brazil and Russia, not to speak of China, the percentages were even lower. *Contingent Reserve Arrangement (CRA)---Impacto para o Brasil*, table 1.

countries of our constituency in the institution to construct a small reserve pooling arrangement, baptized Plurilateral Financing Arrangement (PFA) and based on my experience in the construction of the CRA.[34] Other BRICS countries could have been subsequently invited to participate, although the PFA would have no link to the CRA itself. This was an attempt to take up my original approach to reserve pooling, described above,[35] that focused on regional arrangements centered on the BRICS countries, now targeting, however, not South America but Brazil's IMF constituency, composed almost exclusively of small countries in Latin American and the Caribbean. This would have the advantage of excluding large South American countries that were conducting problematic economic policies, notably Venezuela and Argentina, and that could perhaps have been sources of heavy requests on the arrangement. It would also have considerably strengthened the Brazilian chair in the IMF Board. One source of inspiration for the PFA was the Eurasian Anti-Crisis Fund (ACF), sponsored by Russia. The projected size of the arrangement, US$ 5 billion, as well as Brazil's share, 90 percent, were based largely on the corresponding figures for the ACF, at the time at US$ 8.5 billion, with Russia accounting for 93 percent of the total.[36]

This roundabout way of expanding the approach adopted in the CRA did not work either. The reception among almost all the countries of the constituency was excellent, as could be expected, but the Brazilian Central Bank torpedoed the initiative.[37]

---

34. The PFA would be small for Brazil but significant for the much smaller countries of our constituency in the IMF (Ecuador, Guyana, Suriname, Trinidad and Tobago, Haiti, Dominican Republic, Panama, Nicaragua, Cabo Verde, and Timor-Leste). Ecuador, Panama, and Timor-Leste, with dollarized economies, as well as Haiti, with practically no international reserves except those provided by foreign financial assistance, were excluded from some of the calculations and did not take part in all of the preliminary discussions in the constituency. On the PFA, see *Preliminary Discussions on a Constituency-Based Plurilateral Financing Arrangement (PFA)*, Power Point Presentation, Office of the Executive Director (BR), International Monetary Fund, Technical Meeting, IMF headquarters, Washington, DC, September 11, 2013; and "PFA—Nota Pres Tombini", OEDBR, Washington, DC, 2013. Both documents available at https://www.nogueirabatista.com.br/category/documentos/fmi/.
35. See above, pp. 14 and 15.
36. "PFA—Nota Pres Tombini", pp. 1–4, tables 1, 2, and 3. The ACF had six members at the time (Russia, Armenia, Belarus, Kazakhstan, Kyrgyzstan, and Tajikistan). "PFA—Nota Pres Tombini", table 1.
37. In spite of the fact that I imported from the CRA negotiations all the features that safeguarded the main providing parties—in the case of the PFA, Trinidad and Tobago and, especially, Brazil—including the IMF link for access beyond a certain threshold. We proposed that this threshold be 20 percent of total access for the PFA ("PFA—Nota

Frozen in size and number of members, the CRA failed as well to establish its surveillance unit or permanent secretariat. By contrast, the above-mentioned Chiang Mai Initiative's independent regional surveillance unit, headquartered in Singapore, the ASEAN + 3 Macroeconomic Research Office (AMRO), has become in the meantime a full-fledged international organization carrying out macroeconomic surveillance, supporting the implementation of the Chiang Mai Initiative, and providing technical assistance to members.[38]

In so far as I know, no swap operations were done in the first five years of the CRA's existence. Swaps may have happened without any public information, but this seems unlikely. On this point, the CRA is similar to Chiang Mai, where transparency is also limited, and no lending or swap operations seem to have occurred.

The CRA did not remain, however, completely frozen. Operational procedures have been fully worked out by the Central Banks. CRA governors and officials of the CRA's Standing Committee continue to meet regularly. Three test runs were undertaken, in 2018, 2019, and 2020, to ensure the mechanism's readiness in case of a call on resources.[39] The Brasília BRICS Leaders' Summit declaration welcomed the conclusion of the CRA's second test run, with added elements of complexity, of the delinked portion of the arrangement, including encashment.[40] A system of exchange of information was established in 2017—called the CRA System of Exchange in Macroeconomic Information (SEMI)[41]—perhaps an embryo of a future surveillance unit.

Pres Tombini", p. 3 and table 4), lower than the 30 percent that we were striving for and eventually obtained in the CRA.

38. Each member of the Chiang Mai Initiative is represented in AMRO's Executive Committee by a deputy finance minister and a deputy governor of the Central Bank, with the exception of Hong Kong, special administrative region of China, that is represented by only one deputy. ASEAN + 3 Macroeconomic Research Office, *Governance—Executive Committee*, https://www.amro-asia.org/about-amro/who-we-are/executive-committee/. This is yet another example of the role played by Finance Ministries in initiatives of this type.

39. *Joint Statement on BRICS Leaders' Informal Meeting on the Margins of the G20 Summit*, Osaka, Japan, June 28, 2019, paragraph 10. *Twelfth BRICS Summit—Moscow Declaration*, Moscow, Russia, November 17, 2020, paragraph 61.

40. *Eleventh BRICS Summit—Brasília Declaration*, Brasília, Brazil, November 14, 2019, paragraph 34.

41. *Joint Statement*, Osaka, paragraph 10. *Ninth BRICS Summit—BRICS Leaders' Xiamen Declaration*, September 4, 2017, paragraph 30. The latter also refers to an agreement to further strengthen the CRA's research capability, and to promote closer cooperation between the CRA and the IMF. *Ninth BRICS Summit—BRICS Leaders' Xiamen Declaration*, paragraph 30.

Chapter 4

THE NEW DEVELOPMENT BANK—NDB, ORIGINS AND NEGOTIATIONS

The creation of a development bank by the BRICS goes back to a proposal made by economists Joseph Stiglitz, Nicholas Stern, Amar Bhattacharya, and Mattia Romani to the Indian Prime Minister Manmohan Singh and Indian government officials with whom they had developed close relations.[1] The idea of a new bank was well received when the Indian government brought it to the other BRICS, with the exception of Russia, as noted above. Despite Russia, an understanding was reached. At the level of the Leaders' Summit, in New Delhi, on March 2012, it was Putin who came into play and the Indian proposal was adopted with the inclusion in the Leaders' communiqué of the following crucial sentences that indicated not an agreement to create, or even to start negotiations, but to look into the issue:

> We have considered the possibility of setting up a new Development Bank for mobilizing resources for infrastructure and sustainable development projects in BRICS and other emerging economies and developing countries, to supplement the existing efforts of multilateral and regional financial institutions for global growth and development. We direct our Finance Ministers to examine the feasibility and viability of such an initiative, set up a joint working group for further study, and report back to us by the next Summit.

I draw the reader's attention to one specific point that would become a controversial one later on: the idea from the very beginning was not to create a bank exclusively for the BRICS but one dedicated to supporting development also

1. On the origins of the NDB, see presentation made by Nicholas Stern on the occasion of his visit to the Bank in Shanghai: *NDB—Origins, Opportunities and Challenges*, prepared with Amar Bhattacharya, London School of Economics and Political Science/Grantham Research Institute for Climate Change and the Environment, March 2016, pp. 3–5, available at https://www.nogueirabatista.com.br/category/documentos/brics/ndb/.

in other EMDCs beyond BRICS. After the bank was created, as we will later see, Russian officials would argue repeatedly that the bank had to focus on the BRICS themselves and acted so as to keep it closed to new members in the initial five years of its existence.

A working group was created, cochaired by India and South Africa. One year later, the decision was taken, in the Durban Summit, to start formal negotiations,[2] and the working group was then transformed into a negotiating group. However, the process started off rather poorly. Participants got lost initially in discussing more or less academic papers and notes, not always of high quality, about development banks and related topics. By mid-2013, more than one year after the creation of the working group and months after the Durban decision to create the NDB, nothing much had been done. This was perhaps partly due to Russian obstruction until Durban, but I believe the cochairs were mostly at fault—in the CRA, after all, Russian resistance did not impede us from making progress in the same period.

The picture was not encouraging, when the BRICS finance ministers and negotiating groups met on the sidelines of a G20 meeting in Moscow, in July 2013. Now, in the meantime, I had persuaded almost all the entire relevant parts of the Brazilian government—not only the finance minister, Guido Mantega, but also the minister of foreign relations, Antonio Patriota, as well as the Brazilian Sherpa and Sous Sherpa for the BRICS process and the diplomats that actually took part in the NDB negotiations, Carlos Cozendey and Fernando Pimentel—that it would be not only politically desirable but also technically feasible to conclude the CRA and NDB negotiations by mid-2014 so as to have both agreements signed in Brazil.[3] Guido Mantega in turn easily persuaded President Rousseff of the advantage of having both agreements signed under her chairpersonship.

I was thus somewhat alarmed to see the level of unpreparedness of the NDB at the time, more than one year after the process was launched in Delhi and with one year to go to the Fortaleza Summit. The NDB was way behind the CRA negotiations that were, as we saw, under Brazilian leadership. I reported the situation to Minister Mantega and took the floor in the NDB negotiating meeting in Moscow, although I was not formally a member of the group and only an observer. I explained to the negotiators, who received well my intervention, how we were conducting work in the CRA group. Not by discussing

---

2. *Statement of the BRICS Leaders on the Establishment of the BRICS-Led Development Bank*, Durban, South Africa, March 27, 2013.
3. The reluctance I had to overcome on the part of some of these officials was the simple fear of creating an expectation that could perhaps not be met, risking the wrath of President Rousseff.

papers and vague ideas but actual drafts of the agreement, which later would later take the form of a Treaty. My office in the IMF had actually begun producing draft agreements for discussion in the CRA working group even before the Durban decision to create the arrangement. We proceeded, step by step, meaning that once a specific Article was agreed, the Brazilian CRA chair resisted strenuously, and mostly with success, attempts to reopen settled issues. I explained all this to the NDB negotiators, hoping to help them get their act together. Brazilian diplomats in the Finance Ministry, also taking the cue from how the Brazilian office in the IMF had based the drafts of the CRA on legal and other documents of existing institutions (the IMF, the Chiang Mai Initiative,[4] as well as bilateral swap agreements between central banks), belatedly suggested that the NDB group adopt the same approach, borrowing from the Articles of Agreement of existing multilateral development banks (MDBs), not only the World Bank, the Inter-American Development Bank (IDB) or the Asian Development Bank (ADB) and the African Development Bank (AfDB) but also, interestingly, from Cooperación Andina de Fomento, Development Bank of Latin America (CAF)—a successful regional development bank, flexible and quick in its operations, that would become a source of inspiration for us at the NDB, even beyond the actual drafting of the Articles of Agreement.

From then on, work on the NDB took off. I add right away that when I later moved to Shanghai, as vice president of the Bank, I noticed on repeated occasions that the Articles of Agreement had been well constructed and did not hamper, actually helped considerably, the development of the NDB in practice.

From what I have just written, the reader should take away that Brazil in the period up to our 2015/2016 economic and political crisis often was the real engine of the BRICS and of the NDB negotiations in particular. And this despite the relative meagerness of the number of officials directly involved. Unfortunately, the Brazilian NDB negotiators did not seek or could not obtain support from the Brazilian office in the World Bank. And my repeated attempts to strengthen the Brazilian side by bringing in the BNDES—the Brazilian national development bank—never succeeded, for the simple reason that Minister Mantega was loath to have officials that did not report to him participate in the negotiations.[5] Brazil would eventually pay a price for these

4. Actually, the Chiang Mai legal documents were only partly available for outside consultations, but the Chinese discreetly passed on to me all the relevant details.

5. Luciano Coutinho, president of the BNDES at the time, with whom I often spoke about this, was ready and even eager to participate. However, the BNDES was at the time under the purview of the Ministry of Development, Industry and Commerce.

weaknesses, and specifically in the outcome of crucial matters only resolved at the last minute, in Fortaleza itself.

As the Fortaleza Summit approached, two major issues remained open: the location of the NDB and the nationality of the first president. China, India, and South Africa wanted to host the Bank. Russia and Brazil did not make an offer. This was a mistake on our part and left Brazil without negotiation chips. Shanghai made by far the best offer in financial and other terms. India, the country that had initiated the process, complained astutely that it was not getting headquarters and insisted that it should appoint the first president of the Bank. President Dilma Rousseff was furious at the Brazilian diplomats for not having solved the issue beforehand and for leaving us in a weak negotiating position. She threatened to simply delay the signing of the Agreement.

In Fortaleza, I was among those that argued that it was better not to delay the signature of the Agreement and to give in to India's desire (and the Brazilian chief negotiator, Carlos Cozendey, thanked me heartfeltly for this, since President Dilma was quite a force to reckon with). The following package was then agreed, largely in the ministerial meeting in Fortaleza, one day ahead of the Summit itself. The Bank would be located in Shanghai.[6] India would appoint the first president and Brazil, the second. The order of rotation in the presidency of the NDB would be India, Brazil, Russia, South Africa and, lastly, China,[7] given that Shanghai had obtained headquarters.

South Africa, not having been successful in its bid for headquarters, managed to ensure that the first regional office of the NDB would be located in Johannesburg.[8] This first office would be theoretically responsible for operations not only in South Africa but in the entire African continent. The subsequent regional offices would be established, it was agreed, in Brazil, Russia, and India, as needed.[9] The second one, to be located in Brazil, would be theoretically responsible for the NDB's operations in the Americas. When I say "theoretically" for the first two regional offices I am pointing to a major difficulty that would arise subsequently—the never intended incapacity of the NDB to expand membership beyond BRICS during its first five years.

Brazil also obtained the right to chair the nonresident Board of Directors for the initial four years of the Bank, and Russia the right to be the first chair of the Board of Governors.[10] This would serve us (meaning by "us" here Brazil

6. Article 4 (a) of the *Articles of Agreement of the New Development Bank*, Fortaleza, Brazil, July 15, 2014 (henceforth AoA).
7. *Agreed Minutes of the BRICS Ministerial Meeting*, Fortaleza, Brazil, July 15, 2014 (henceforth Agreed Minutes), first paragraph.
8. Article 4 (b) of the AoA.
9. *Agreed Minutes*, third paragraph.
10. *Sixth BRICS Summit—Fortaleza Declaration*, Fortaleza, Brazil, July 15, 2014, paragraph 12.

as well as the NDB) better than I expected in Fortaleza, for the reason that initially Brazil was represented in the Board of Directors by two experienced and intelligent diplomats, Luís Balduino, as director, and Carlos Cozendey, who had been the chief negotiator for Brazil in the NDB negotiations, as alternate director. Unfortunately, this would only last until late 2016, when the Temer government replaced these diplomats by somewhat second-rate economists that had little or no experience with multilateral negotiations.

With the benefit of hindsight, I must say that the stance I took in Fortaleza was mistaken. Shanghai would prove indeed an excellent place to locate the Bank, but India chose a weak first president for the first five years of the NDB, K. V. Kamath, an illustrious name from the private sector but in preretirement mode and not at all inclined to take the NDB project to heart, as I will explain subsequently. Perhaps even more problematic, leaving the second president to Brazil would hand the choice to the Bolsonaro Administration, the worst government the country has ever had, I venture to say. But, of course, who could imagine that Brazil would go down that route back then, when the decision was taken in July 2014? Had I known, I would have suggested that my country appoint the third or the fourth president!

The NDB begins in Shanghai

The NDB is undoubtedly the main practical achievement of the BRICS process, more important than the CRA, since it was planned to become an actual institution with substantial paid-in capital, a sufficiently large staff, and the capacity to leverage capital by borrowing in the markets, as MDBs always do, since the creation of the first one, the World Bank. The NDB can actually turn out to be one of the largest MDBs in the world. By 2022, its paid-in capital will have reached US$ 10 billion if the founding members comply with what is set out in the Articles of Agreement. With new members, paid-in capital could easily reach a considerably higher level. At the time of the NDB's creation, the ADB's paid-in capital was US$ 7 billion, the IDB's, US$ 6 billion, and the AfDB's, US$ 5 billion. The World Bank had US$ 16 billion and faced considerable difficulties in expanding its capital base due to the resistance of many of its major shareholders. It should be noted, moreover, that the NDB is the first large MDB created exclusively by emerging market countries, without participation of advanced countries in the initial stage. Also significantly, it is the first MDB since the World Bank to be established with a global mandate, that is, with the intention of bringing in members from and operating in all regions of the world.

With such ambitious plans, it was no surprise that the NDB was received with concern in Washington, by the US government, as well as the Administration of the Washington-based institutions, particularly the World Bank. This was also true of the CRA to a lesser extent. It was feared that the World Bank might perhaps suffer from the competition of the NDB over time. And Christine Lagarde, the managing director of the IMF at the time, was also initially surprised by the creation of the CRA and sought to obtain information about it from me and the other executive directors of BRICS countries in the IMF Board.

Experience would show, however, that these concerns were exaggerated. Despite some progress, the CRA remained largely frozen after 2015, as explained above, and from Shanghai there was nothing I could possibly do. The NDB would struggle to get its act together, despite my efforts. Jim O'Neill, the creator of the BRICs acronym, was right to say, in November 2018, that "the BRICS bank has been a disappointment so far—almost anonymous." The observation remains true two years later at the time of writing of this book.

Why did this happen? The problem has two dimensions, I believe. First, internal problems of the Bank, especially the weaknesses of the NDB's first Administration, composed of the president and four vice presidents. Second, and perhaps more importantly, a macropolitical one, related to developments, political and economic, in the BRICS countries and in their international relations. I will address them in turn.

Before going into these dimensions, I provide a brief description of the NDB's governance, of what seemed to be promising first steps, from mid-2015 to mid-2016, and of the Bank's General Strategy for 2017–21.[11]

Governance and first steps

The NDB's governance, as defined in the Articles of Agreement, is on the whole very traditional—no surprise given the way they were drafted. The Board of Governors, responsible for matters of strategic importance, is the highest authority, composed of governors and alternate governors designated

11. A version in Portuguese of the following five sections of this book can be found in the book I published at the end of 2019. Paulo Nogueira Batista Jr., *O Brasil não cabe no quintal de ninguém: bastidores da vida de um economista brasileiro no FMI e nos BRICS e outros textos sobre nacionalismo e nosso complexo de vira-lata*, São Paulo, LeYa, 2019, pp. 256–83. What follows is to a large extent an English translation of this text, partly rewritten and directed more at the non-Brazilian reader. Additional elements were added here, especially an update on further developments in the NDB in the second half of 2019 and the first half of 2020. A discussion of the NDB's origins, governance, and initial steps can also be found in Luciana Acioly da Silva, *Arquitetura Financeira Conjunta do BRICS: O Novo Banco de Desenvolvimento*, Texto para Discussão 2463, Instituto de Pesquisa Econômica Aplicada—IPEA, Rio de Janeiro, March 2019.

by the member countries, the governors being necessarily of ministerial rank.[12] All five founding members chose to be represented in this Board by their finance ministers. The Board of Directors, responsible for conducting the ordinary business of the Bank, is made up mostly of mid-level officials from the Finance Ministries of the countries. The Administration of the Bank—the president, initially from India, and four vice presidents, from the BRICS countries other than the country appointing the president—reside in Shanghai and are the ones actually leading the work of the Bank, under the supervision of both Boards. The workload and responsibilities were divided by topic among the president and the four vice presidents. The Brazilian vice president, for instance, became responsible for risk, strategy, partnerships, economic research, and expansion of membership.

This is all relatively humdrum. However, the reader should notice two important singularities of the NDB's governance. First, the fact that the Board of Directors is a nonresident body. This is exceedingly rare in international financial institutions, almost all of which have resident Boards, as is the case of the Boards of the World Bank, the ADB, the IDB, the AfDB, and the IMF, of which I had been a member. The Asian Infrastructure Investment Bank (AIIB), created under Chinese leadership shortly after the NDB, also opted for a nonresident Board.[13] I will not go into the discussion of the advantages and disadvantages of resident and nonresident Boards, a debate that goes back to John Maynard Keynes and Harry Dexter White and the creation of the Bretton Woods institutions.[14] For the purposes of the present discussion, I need only mention that resident Boards are better at controlling and supervising the work of the Administration. The NDB would suffer to some extent

12. Article 11 (a) of the AoA.
13. According to Christopher Humphrey, the preference of European shareholders of AIIB was a resident Board of Directors, but China insisted on a nonresident Board. Christopher Humphrey, *From Drawing Board to Reality: The First Four Years of Operations of the Asian Infrastructure Investment Bank and New Development Bank*, Working Paper of the G-24 and Global Development Policy Center of Boston University, April 2020, pp. 3 and 29. Incidentally, the Germans went around this by having their "nonresident" director work in Beijing from the German Embassy, as I was told by the country's Ambassador to China.
14. See, for example, Roy Harrod, *The Life of John Maynard Keynes*. New York: W.W. Norton, 1982 (first edition: 1951), pp. 632–35; and Leonardo Martinez-Diaz, *Executive Boards in International Organizations: Lessons for Strengthening IMF Governance*. Independent Evaluation Office of the IMF, IEO Background Paper, BP/08/08, revised May 2008, p. 16. See, also, Paulo Nogueira Batista Jr., *O Brasil não cabe no quintal de ninguém*, pp. 62–63 and 258–59. The AoA explicitly foresaw the possibility of creating a resident Board, in which case the president of the NDB would become the chairperson. Article 12 (g) of the AoA.

from the excessive freedom given, in practice, to a relatively incompetent first Administration.

A second singularity of the NDB's governance is the equal distribution of capital and voting power among the five founding members. None of the major international financial institutions display this feature. During the negotiations, China tried to have the lion's share of capital and votes, but the other countries managed to rebuff the aspiration. In the NDB, no country plays the leading role that the United States plays in the IMF and the World Bank. Or that China plays in the AIIB. In these organizations, the United States or China have veto power over crucial decisions. As in the CRA, the NDB negotiators sought to avoid giving veto power to any of the members, with more success in this respect than we had in the CRA negotiations. In the NDB, no decisions at all require consensus in the sense of unanimity since this would amount to giving veto power to each and every member. All decisions were designed to be taken by simple majority or by supermajorities. Unfortunately, this good design did not really work, a point to which I will come back. The president of the Bank allowed the practice to be established that decisions would be taken by consensus in virtually all cases. Thus, the NDB would end up with five "USAs" in practice, a rather terrible scenario.

When I arrived in Shanghai, we were starting literally from scratch. We basically had the Articles of Agreement and an empty floor of a building in Lujiazui, the financial district of Shanghai. Quite depressing, as I recall. I sometimes regretted having accepted the task. Moving to the other side of the world, to a strange country, with a language I did not speak, was not at all easy after eight years in Washington, away from home and family in Brazil. I had no team, not even administrative assistants, initially. Our only help were a few Chinese government officials from the central government in Beijing and the municipal government of Shanghai, some of whom, however, spoke little English. I was soon joined by the other four members of the Administration, but they were complete strangers with quite different professional backgrounds. And I would not take long to learn that, with the exception of the Chinese vice president, none of the others were truly fit for the job.

It took us one or two months to get going and initial results did seem promising. The NDB's first year, up to mid-2016, did not look all that bad. We managed to approve all the main policies of the Bank—lending policies, treasury, administration, risk, environment and social safeguards, human resources, recruitment, among others—even if some of these were weak, hired out to expensive consultants, or largely copied from those of other MDBs. Anyhow, we were moving forward. Paid-in capital was deposited on schedule by member countries, and even in advance by some (China and Russia)—a demonstration of support for the NDB.

Another achievement in the first year was the preparation and negotiation of the first batch of projects, one for each of the BRICS, all of them in the area of renewable energy, as had been requested by the Leaders of the BRICS in their Summit in Ufa, Russia, July 2015. The target set by the president of the Bank to carry out in less than six months the evaluation, negotiation, and approval of loans was achieved. In this we were helped by the member countries that in the beginning often provided us projects in an advanced stage of preparations, relatively easy to carry out or at least to bring to the Board of Directors.[15] As I will later show, there was something of make-believe in the way the Bank worked, forgivable in the beginning, but not if lasting for five years as it eventually did.

But let me not get ahead of myself. Suffice to say for now that we managed in the first year to set the NDB clearly as a "green bank", dedicated to environmentally friendly projects and "green" on the funding side as well. Our first bond, issued in July 2016, was a 5-year "green bond", denominated in renminbi, for 3 billion (equivalent to about US$ 450 million at the time).[16] The issuance was remarkably successful, with the bond being oversubscribed more than three times and the coupon at 3.07 percent, only slightly above the interest rate paid by China Development Bank at the time. This success reflected initial optimism with the NDB but could hardly be attributed to merits of the Administration. The reason for the successful issuance was the strong support from China, meaning not only the central government in Beijing but also the municipal government in Shanghai, and the Chinese commercial and investment banks, all of them public. The Chinese economic and political army, in short, went to war for us.

In the first year, therefore, the NDB managed, consistent with its mandate, to present itself as a green bank, on the lending and funding side. At one point, the Bank was 100 percent green on both sides of its balance sheet, quite an

15. In the case of Brazil, the project was a two-step loan with BNDES for renewable energy projects. In the case of Russia, the financing of a small hydroelectric power plant in Karelia through two international financial institutions dominated by Russia, the Eurasian Development Bank (EDB) and the International Investment Bank (IIB). New Development Bank, *List of All Projects*, http//www.ndb.int. The unusual format of the first Russian project arose from the fact that the country's national development bank, Vnesheconombank—VEB, was on the list of entities sanctioned by the United States and other countries. The NDB initially sought to work with VEB, but later realized the risks involved and a roundabout way was found to avoid falling victim to Western sanctions. I will come back below to the wider consequences for the NDB of the sanctions imposed on Russia after 2014.

16. New Development Bank, *Annual Report 2019: Innovation for Innovation*, p. 55, http//www.ndb.int.

achievement of which I was initially proud. Time would show that this was also partly illusory.

General strategy and plans for expansion of membership

In parallel to these operational activities, we prepared the strategy of the Bank for the 2017–21 period, simultaneously with the plans and procedures for the entry of new members. In the area of strategy, the work of the NDB was more original than in the other areas, despite resistance of some bureaucrats in the capitals of the BRICS to anything that smacked of originality, as bureaucrats are often prone to. After prolonged and detailed discussions inside the Bank, with the Board of Governors, and mostly the Board of Directors, the strategy document was approved in principle in April 2017—nearly two years after the beginning of our work in Shanghai.[17] The strategy and the expansion of membership were under the purview of governors,[18] but since they were all finance ministers, with not too much time to spare for the NDB, these issues fell to the level of the Board of Directors in practice, unhappily so, since mid-level government officials, not always, but often, failed to display the high-level political and strategic vision required to address these matters. Moreover, in some cases, they feared accepting proposals that might in the end be rejected by their ministers and leaders with unpredictable consequences for their careers in government. This seemed to be especially true for Russia, a point to which I will return.

Expansion of membership proved to be remarkably difficult, much more than I expected. The fact that the matter, although under the purview of governors, fell to the level of directors had even worse consequences than for the strategy. In 2016 and 2017, preliminary contacts were made with about 70 countries from all regions of the world to sound out possible interest in joining the NDB. We were well received in most cases, but Russian objections and maneuvers against expansion of membership delayed everything. Every step we took was taken in the teeth of severe Russian resistance. Having successfully contained and defeated Napoleon and Hitler, the Russians were, the reader will realize, a force that we could not underestimate! The matter, as

17. Final approval by the Board of Governors happened in July 2017, after some additional adjustments to the text. The document can be found in the NDB's website: *NDB's General Strategy: 2017–2021*, http//www.ndb.int.

18. Admittance of new members and the determination of the conditions for their admission are among the powers of the Board of Governors that cannot be delegated to directors. Article 11 (b) of the AoA. In practice, the matter was mostly discussed with directors, with final decisions taken by governors.

mentioned, was handled by the Brazilian vice-presidency and I had to struggle every small step of the way. The weakness and lack of ambition of the president, always fearful of any confrontation, made everything extremely difficult. The other members of the Administration, with the exception of the Chinese vice president, did not help but actually hindered.[19] In any case, to the displeasure of the Russians, we managed to initiate contacts and to approve the terms, conditions, and procedures for the admission of new members.[20]

Innovation was the central principle of the NDB's General Strategy for 2017–21. The starting point was the overall model inaugurated by the World Bank in Bretton Woods, with national governments pooling their resources so as to leverage capital to support reconstruction after the Second World War and, later, economic and social development in EMDCs. We were not arrogant fools and recognized that a lot had to be learned from existing MDBs, not only the World Bank itself but also from the many regional MDBs, as well as from our own national development banks, especially the Chinese and Brazilian ones.[21] We came to sign many cooperation and partnership agreements with these institutions, although largely because of NDB's own limitations, we often did not take full advantage of this. However, we never lost sight—at least in the initial years, for the duration of my stay there—of the need to seek a new approach and new practices. After all, why would the BRICS have gone to all the trouble and expense of creating their own MDB if they had been fully satisfied with the existing ones? This may seem obvious to the reader, but he or she should realize how easy it was to depart from fundamental goals in the day-to-day activities of building a bank from scratch, the more so that my colleagues in the Administration had had no participation in the BRICS process up to then.

---

19. Not only the Russian but also the South African vice president created difficulties for the admittance of new members, the latter with the unpersuasive argument that expansion of membership, as then envisaged by us, would hurt the NDB's debut credit rating. More on that below.
20. New Development Bank, *Terms, Conditions and Procedures for the Admission of New Members*, http//www.ndb.int. Discussions of the strategy and plans for membership expansion proceeded on the basis of drafts and revisions prepared by the Brazilian vice-presidency. The several rounds of contacts with potential new members were also organized by us. I counted for this on a small team of which Zhan Shu and Fabio Batista, especially the latter, were the outstanding participants. Particularly important for the elaboration of the strategy document was the contribution of an external consultant: Christopher Humphrey, one of the most experienced researchers on MDBs.
21. India had no national development bank. The Russian and South African ones, despite our willingness to interact and their readiness to cooperate, seemed to have less to offer in terms of experience and track record.

The General Strategy adopted, implicitly, a Taoist principle that I took from my (mostly unsuccessful) efforts to understand Chinese Ancient Philosophy: "Concepts exist only as contrasts."[22] The plans of the new institution were presented, generally speaking, in contrast to the way the existing MDBs worked. The language was diplomatic, but the message was clear: our intention was to depart from traditional practices that seemed outdated or problematic from the point of view of EMDCs. It may be worthwhile to summarize these intended innovations, although most of them remained on paper, for reasons to be explained later on.

So, what would be new in the New Development Bank? How would it become a truly new multilateral institution, worthy of its name? That was the question we explicitly asked ourselves and in the strategy document. Idealistic? No doubt. And this line of thinking was silently, sometimes not so silently, rejected by pragmatists in the Administration and in the Board, worried basically about their own jobs and skeptical of big ideas. The idealists had to struggle permanently against these forces of inertia. Now, the Articles of Agreement of NDB had set out as mandate for the Bank to mobilize resources for infrastructure and sustainable development in BRICS and other EMDCs,[23] leaving the precise definition of these terms wide open. The strategy document specified that in the first five-year period, from 2017 to 2021, the NDB would focus on sustainable infrastructure, with two-thirds of approved projects in this area. I met some resistance from the Chinese vice president, in charge of operations, who did not wish to have his hands tied, but in the end he gave in, hoping perhaps that in practice there would be much leeway for operations. And, indeed, "sustainable infrastructure" was flexibly defined as the type of infrastructure that incorporates sustainability criteria in all its phases, from conception to actual operation—and we meant, of course, not only financial and economic but also social and environmental sustainability. Actually, environmental criteria were foremost in our mind. The remaining one-third would include all traditional infrastructure and sustainable development projects not related to infrastructure, such as pollution control, conservation of biodiversity, and adaptation to climate change. The concept of sustainable infrastructure had the advantage for us of blending the two dimensions of the NDB's mandate as set out in the Articles of Agreement.[24]

22. I would have made the principle explicit but ran up against the resistance of others in the Administration and in the Board of Directors. When I quoted it in a Board meeting, I got some impatient or irritated looks from participating officials—the Chinese aside, glad to see their ancient philosophy receive unexpected recognition in what was, as usual, a rather bureaucratic gathering.
23. Article 2 of the AoA.
24. New Development Bank, *NDB's General Strategy: 2017–2021*, pp. 12, 13.

Even in traditional infrastructure projects, NDB would apply, as do or should do all MDBs, social and environmental requirements, so-called safeguards, to control or mitigate any negative effects on social groups and the environment. The difference between traditional and sustainable infrastructure projects, as formulated by us, was that the latter would go beyond mere mitigation of collateral effects in these areas. They would have as their main goal obtaining positive results in social and environmental terms. For this to happen, it was decided that the Bank would focus on sectors such as renewable energy—solar, wind, small dams—energy efficiency, clean transportation, urban mobility, water supply, and sanitation, including solid waste management.

As I write these words, three or four years later, I am overtaken again by the enthusiasm that conducted our work back then. I refer essentially to the Brazilian and Chinese vice-presidencies, as well as some younger officials in other areas of the Bank. It was undoubtedly a beautiful project and many of us were proud to be part of it, even if it meant for the non-Chinese to be very far from home, in a strange and totally different country. In any case, the Chinese in Shanghai, inside and outside the Bank, were normally very receptive to us foreigners, and this made life much more bearable. The younger members of staff, in particular, were easily caught up in the enthusiasm, although this would unfortunately not last.

Existing MDBs were, of course, already operating in the area of sustainable infrastructure and we were not claiming to have invented the wheel. However, the lack of focus of many MDBs, that is, their tendency to operate in a vast number of areas, seemed to harm their effectiveness. This was for us a negative take-away from the experience of our predecessors in the MDB world. The World Bank, in particular, tried to cover all positions, from port and dams to saving the Siberian tiger. The NDB's strategy explicitly stated the intention of avoiding the "universal style" of traditional MDBs in favor of focusing our energy on a more limited set of sectors, even if sufficiently wide to allow us to find viable projects.[25]

The NDB's strategy document also proclaimed the intention to incorporate speed in all its activities. The idea was to combine the speed and efficiency of the private sector with the technical rigor, high quality, and commitment to the public good that characterize MDBs. We wrote this a little tongue-in-cheek but meant it essentially. The first part of the sentence harked back to the experience of the president in a private Indian bank, the second part to that of the Chinese vice president, with a long background in the MDB world. In

25. Ibid., p. 12.

theory, not a bad combination. Practice would prove to be an entirely different matter.

We realized that to some extent, but declared, anyway, our intention to avoid "unnecessary bureaucracy" in the approval and implementation of projects, allowing the NDB to achieve the already mentioned goal of taking less than six months, on average, between the identification of projects and their approval by the Board of Directors.[26] A goal the Bank would meet in a formal sense, especially in the beginning, but rarely in practice, for reasons I will explain later on. This six-month target was considerably lower than what was observed at the time in older MDBs, such as the World Bank and the IDB.[27]

Another important goal was to lend, as much as possible, in the national currencies of member countries, so as to avoid exchange rate risk for the borrowers and, even if only marginally in the beginning, to contribute to the development of domestic capital markets. Experience showed that the more common practice among MDBs of lending in US dollars created recurrent difficulties in the implementation of projects. I note in passing that this goal was not primarily motivated by any wish on our part of displacing the dollar or reducing its role in international markets—the NDB was in any case too small for that, and would remain so for a long time. Our concern was of an essentially practical nature. Infrastructure and sustainable development projects are typically long term and borrowers find it normally difficult to hedge exchange risks for long maturities at an affordable cost. Moreover, most of these projects are in non-tradeable sector of the economy and do not supply the natural hedge associated with gains from export earnings or from substituting imports in case of a devaluation. To make this viable for the NDB, our plan was to de-dollarize part of our funding in capital markets and explore possibilities of funding in national currencies of members. The process had indeed already begun with the successful issuance of the bond in Chinese currency.

It could be said, therefore, that things did not look all that bad for the NDB in the beginning. The strategy document was at pains to stress that we would depart from what we thought was the interventionist and salvationist model of some of the traditional MDBs, notably the World Bank, often prone to excessive meddling in the borrowing countries. Again, we adopted diplomatic language, partly because of concerns from capitals about what was seen as

26. Ibid., pp. 3, 10, and 15.
27. See, for instance, Christopher Humphrey, *Infrastructure Finance in the Developing World: Challenges and Opportunities for Multilateral Development Banks in 21st Century Infrastructure Finance*, Intergovernmental Group of Twenty-Four and Global Green Growth Institute, Working Paper Series, June 2015, section 4.1.

excessive novelty in the first drafts of the strategy that came from the Brazilian vice-presidency. In any case, it was left abundantly clear that we would not attempt to teach or preach to borrowing countries nor impose conditionality of any sort. On the contrary, the NDB would respect the priorities and national strategies of borrowing countries, maintaining a relation of equality, mutual respect, and trust with member countries—an approach that was supposed to permeate all our policies and operations.[28] We would start whenever possible from the laws and national procedures of countries in the implementation of projects—and not try to impose our own blueprint on them.[29]

I hope the reader is not running out of patience with fine words and intentions. I am soon coming to what actually happened in real life. But before that, a word on plans for the expansion of membership. This was crucial for a bank that intended to be global in nature. Our plans for this were ambitious but gradualist. I would have acted quicker but had no support for that, especially from the president, who was slow and had inordinate difficulty in taking decisions that could be risky in the slightest way. So we (reluctantly) explained in the strategy document that the first two years of the NDB, from mid-2015 to mid-2017, had been dedicated to consolidating the institution, including approving basic operational policies, hiring initial staff, receiving the first installments of paid-in capital from founding members, and issuing the first bond. This decision was taken, we stated in the document, to facilitate the elaboration of policies that would allow us to be a fundamentally different institution compared to older MDBs.[30] The explanation was not entirely persuasive, I can now say. This would perhaps be a reason for delaying the entry of pushy large advanced countries but was no reason not to bring in as soon as possible other EMDCs and smaller advanced countries.

The NDB, as stated in the General Strategy, expected to influence the international financial architecture and global practices. To achieve this, we noted, the Bank had to operate at scale and that meant expanding membership beyond the BRICS, with the following advantages, among others: (1) enhancement of the institution's profile and international standing; (2) diversification of its sphere of operations to more countries, reducing portfolio concentration; (3) increase in paid-in capital; and (4) leveraging the experience of other countries in project design and implementation.[31] To non-borrowing

28. New Development Bank, *NDB's General Strategy*, pp. 4, 11, 15 and 16.

29. In each project, the NDB would check *ex ante* the quality and reliability of the borrowing country's systems in environmental, social, procurement, and fiduciary areas. If these systems were considered insufficient, the NDB would define additional requirements, adapted to the specific needs of each project. Ibid., pp. 15 and 16.

30. Ibid., pp. 4, 26, and 34.

31. Ibid., p. 26.

advanced countries, it was noted, joining the NDB could be particularly attractive to those that focus on promoting infrastructure and sustainable development in the developing world and to those that also wished to give their firms access to procurement opportunities in the NDB.[32]

We believed in mid-2017 (wrongly, as it turned out) that plans for expansion of membership could finally begin to be implemented. The idea was to incorporate in stages countries of different size, levels of development, and regions of the world, ensuring geographic diversity and a reasonable mix of advanced, middle-income, and lower-income countries.[33] Gradually, NDB would receive new member countries from Asia, the Americas, Africa, Middle East, Europe, and Oceania. After the five-year period covered by the strategy paper, the NDB would have become a global bank present in all regions of the world.[34] Nothing of the sort ever happened during the five-years of the Kamath presidency from July 2015 to July 2020. And the NDB remains to this day a five-country closed club, although plans to expand membership remain on the table.

As a cynic might well note, and a saying goes in Brazil, "paper accepts anything." Nevertheless, the fact that the strategy document, as well as the ones related to new members, had been negotiated step by step with the Board of Governors, and practically paragraph by paragraph with the Board of Directors, held up the expectation that there was real commitment on the part of the founding members to what was in the end approved by governors. Moreover, all five members of the Administration had been involved in the discussion, and the document was not something up in the air but deliberately reflected what we were actually doing in practice since July 2015.

This expectation was largely unfounded. The goals set out in the strategy were not unrealistic, nor excessively ambitious, but many of them proved to be way beyond the Bank's actual capacity for reasons that I now turn to.

Internal problems of the NDB

As time went by, it became clear to me that the Administration of the Bank was not up to the challenge with which it was confronted. There was to begin with no true adherence of most of its members to the project that the NDB was supposed to incarnate. I was, as already mentioned, the only one of the

32. Ibid., p. 26. As per Article 21 (vi) of the AoA, funds provided by the NDB can only be used for procurement of goods and services produced in member countries. Exceptions may be permitted by the Board of Directors in special circumstances.
33. Ibid., p. 26.
34. Ibid., pp. 4 and 34.

five that had taken part in the BRICS process and to have an experience-based understanding of what our countries originally wished to achieve with the creation of a new institution. The Chinese vice president, Zhu Xian, came from a long career in the ADB and the World Bank and was a valuable addition to the Administration, being well acquainted with the pluses and minuses of these and other MDBs. An intelligent professional, he fully realized the NDB's incipient problems, about which we often spoke, sharing our increasing frustration. He was in charge of the crucial area of projects and also of the supervision of the regional offices created by the Bank. But he was an exception, unfortunately.

The other members of the Administration left much to be desired. Lack of the required sense of mission was not the only problem. The South African and Russian vice presidents were not qualified for the job. Leslie Maasdorp, the South African in charge of Treasury, Portfolio Management, Finance, Budget and Accounting, had insufficient technical knowledge, little administrative capacity, and often abandoned his responsibilities, spending excessive time with travel and events. The Russian vice president, Vladimir Kazbekov, was an even worse case. Before coming to Shanghai, he had been for a long time a mid-level official in Russia's national development bank, responsible for international relations and organization of events. In NDB, he was charged with Human Resources, Communication, Administration, Information Technology and Security. All these areas suffered from his lack of professional competence. For example, all sectors of the Bank were more or less strangled from lack of human resources—including HR itself. Recruitment was slow, inefficient and lacked transparency. The staff that we hired was of uneven quality. Communication also worked poorly. To this day, the NDB has little public presence and is almost unknown, "anonymous", as Jim O'Neill noted.

The main problem, however, was the president of the Bank, K. V. Kamath. Although an intelligent and experienced professional, with a background in commercial banking in India, he probably saw the NDB as the final step in his career and showed limited commitment to the institution. A poor communicator, he made little effort to draw attention to the Bank and did not bother to establish or strengthen external contacts. He showed little enthusiasm for the NDB as a project, often giving the impression that he was counting the days to the end of his mandate. He was easily intimidated and rarely risked taking sides on difficult matters. With this profile, he could of course not exercise authority and leadership. My efforts and those of the Chinese vice president were not enough to compensate for the weaknesses of the rest of Management, especially of the president. I was eventually to be replaced by a nondescript and relatively inexperienced Brazilian diplomat, Sarquis Buainain Sarquis, who remained in the Bank until June 2020, and left no achievements to speak of.

The officials in the third and fourth echelons of the governments of the founding members, initially a little in awe of the illustrious Indian banker, did not take long to notice his weakness and started to pressure him mercilessly. To approve the policies and decisions proposed by the Administration of the NDB, they made detailed demands, not always relevant or well thought out. It was never clear whether these mid- or even lower level officials had the backing of higher-level authorities to proceed as they did, but the president did not really try to find out and always made an effort to accommodate in some way the great majority of demands coming from the five capitals, no matter how absurd or off the point.[35]

When the Articles of Agreement were negotiated, I note again, there was a concern of avoiding that decisions in NDB should depend on unanimity or consensus. Thus, the great majority of decisions were to be taken by simple majority, and a few would require a qualified supermajority (two-thirds of voting power) or a special supermajority (four of the founding members plus two-thirds of voting power).[36] As each of the founding members has 20 percent of votes, this means that none of them can exercise veto power over any matter. In practice, however, as mentioned before, the president of the NDB would only take a decision when all five members were on board. Very rarely was anything decided against the opinion of a single member. As a result, matters brought to the Board of Directors and the Board of Governors, even those of lesser importance, tended to drag away incredibly. The speed proclaimed in the strategy document, as well as in pronouncements of the president, became dead letter.

The root of these problems lay in the lack of political acumen of the Indian president. He might have been a good vice president for treasury and budget, certainly better than the one we had, but was not fit for the presidency. It soon became clear that he had trouble dealing with the member countries. During the time I was there, he failed to establish regular contact with finance ministers—exception made to the minister of his own country, India. His interactions with the capitals were limited mostly to the mid-rank officials of the government. The NDB ended up entangled with the bureaucracies of the five countries.

35. There may seem to be a contradiction between the observation that the president was under constant pressure from mid-level bureaucrats and the assessment made earlier (pp.39 and 40) that the nonresident nature of the Board of Directors gave excessive freedom to the Administration. But what happened was that, while members did indeed press for their particular interests and views, they actually exercised poor oversight over the NDB's implementation of policies and day-to-day operations.

36. Article 6 (b) of the AoA. The distinction between these two types of supermajorities will of course only become relevant as membership of the NDB expands.

The contrast with President Jin Liqun of AIIB was embarrassing for us. Created shortly after the NDB, the AIIB has a dynamic and creative president, who led his institution to a prominent role from the very beginning, casting a deep shadow over our bank. In fact, despite its regional focus—the AIIB was intended as an Asian bank that would compete with the ADB where Japan and the United States have prominent positions—the bank headquartered in Beijing increasingly came to play the global role that was intended for the NDB. Early on the AIIB had managed to bring in a large number of countries, including from outside Asia and all major advanced countries with the exceptions of the United States and Japan. Meanwhile, under Kamath's leadership (or lack thereof) the bank created by the BRICS languished. Five years after its operations began in July 2015, no new countries have joined the Bank and plans for expansion of membership have suffered repeated delays. Lack of initiative and leadership on the part of the Indian president was one major reason for this.

The relative lack of success of the NDB cannot be attributed, in my assessment, to a greater support of China to the AIIB. Support from China was always there for the NDB—and by China I mean not only the central government in Beijing but also the powerful municipal government in Shanghai, eager to see the success of the first multilateral international financial institution located in the city. Many of the achievements of the NDB were, in fact, due to the professionally solid and systematic help from the Chinese, not only for the already mentioned first bond issuance but also in other relevant aspects of the Bank's activities.

My own individual position, I must say, was not ideal. I could not claim to be a perfect fit for the job, especially for Risk. I did have a lot of experience and knowledge of multilateral negotiations, of one particular international financial institution, the IMF, and of the BRICS process itself, but no prior practical knowledge of development banks. On-the-job training and studying was therefore required, but this took time and effort. It would have been crucial for me to hire a good director general for Risk but I was hindered in this by the slowness of the Bank's HR and by bad luck in selecting Brazilian candidates that gave up after their names were approved.

My temper did not help either, I must recognize. After some time and repeated frustrations, I reacted with impatience and asperity to the lack of dedication and responsibility of my South African and Russian colleagues. With the Russian vice president, who was not only incompetent but also aggressive, disagreements multiplied and he went so far, believe it or not, as to use his attributions in HR and communications to retaliate against other colleagues, notably against the Brazilian vice-presidency, obstructing our work repeatedly. The Chinese vice president also often lost patience with our Russian and South African colleagues since their poor performance harmed his work in the area of projects and regional centers. The internal meetings of the Administration were often not very constructive, as an old school Englishman would say. The president remained basically inert, mostly shying away from exercising the leadership that was his due.[37]

The limitations of the NDB's leadership contributed to poor decisions in the hiring of staff. The positions of director general and chief, the highest levels of staff, were often taken by persons of insufficient background and competence during my time in Shanghai. The work of the NDB suffered from this in practically all sectors. What saved the situation somewhat was the performance of the Chinese vice president, as well as of some Chinese staff, including those working in my vice-presidency. Moreover, the Brazilians, although few and relatively young and inexperienced, worked well and hard, almost without exception. For these Brazilian and Chinese technical staff, at least those working in the Brazilian vice-presidency, overtime and work on weekends or holidays was routine, and nobody raised an eyebrow. What counted for us was a sense that we were responsible for something unique in the history of our countries, and that we had to behave accordingly and accept exceptional personal sacrifices.

The above scathing criticisms of my former colleagues, especially of the Administration, may sound excessively *ad hominem*. However, one should not lose sight of the fact that the personal qualities of the leadership are crucial for entirely new institutions such as the NDB. An already established and consolidated bank can withstand for some time an ineffective Administration. But the NDB had started literally from scratch and depended critically on the qualities and dedication of the Administration and staff, precisely the qualities and dedication that were sorely missed, especially in the higher echelons of the institution.

---

37. In truth, the Russian vice president mostly behaved, without much disguise and rather crudely, as Russia's resident executive director, and not as a member of the Administration. This behavior was a flagrant violation of the AoA and of the contracts we had signed when we joined the NDB. The AoA established that the president, the vice presidents, and the staff of the Bank, in the discharge of their offices, owe their duty exclusively to the Bank and to no other authority. Article 13 (f) of the AoA. In line with the format usually adopted in multilateral organizations, the contracts of the presidents and vice presidents of the NDB contained similar dispositions. I myself had written the first drafts of these contracts, following to a large extent those of the IMF and the World Bank.

Political setbacks

The NDB's difficulties were not only internal to the Bank. We also had to struggle with developments that affected the international relations, as well as the political and economic situation of the BRICS countries, leading to a number of negative repercussions for the institution. These macro-developments were arguably even more decisive for the Bank than the institution's own limitations.

One of these was the deterioration of relations between China and India. In 2013, China had launched the One Belt, One Road Initiative (OBOR), a series of large-scale infrastructure investments in Asia, Africa, Europe, and other regions. OBOR would, as almost everything else, suffer considerable damage when the pandemic broke out in 2020, but the impetus of the first years, the scale and ambition of Chinese plans, became a source of concern for India, in particular a project for an economic corridor for China/Pakistan, from Tibet to the ports of Karachi and Gwadar, that went through territory contested by India and Pakistan. More broadly, it could be said that China's rise sparked traditional historical rivalries with India that had even led, as is well known, to a war between the two countries in 1962, won by China. India's resentment was a factor that the Chinese should have taken into account and had perhaps failed to do so sufficiently. The United States—even before Trump, consistently interested in benefiting from this discord—tried and sometimes succeeded in attracting India into a quadripartite alliance with Japan and Australia to "contain" China. Scuffles on the China/India frontier occurred in 2017, significantly harming the planning of the BRICS Summit of that year, held in Xiamen, China. Relations improved thereafter but, in 2020, new conflicts occurred in the Himalayas, this time more seriously, with casualties on both sides.

How could this not affect the NDB? Every low point of China/India relations was a risk for the institution, headquartered in China with an Indian president up to mid-2020. For instance, when the Chinese government approached the Bank to request that we sign a Memorandum of Understanding (MoU), together with other MDBs, indicating the intention to support OBOR, India was adamantly opposed, although the MoU was merely declaratory and not legally binding in any way. After many comings and goings, and in cold sweat, Kamath finally put the matter to a vote and India was defeated by 4 to 1. This was the only time, in the more than two years that I worked in the NDB, that any decision was taken without consensus. The reader can imagine the pressure that the Chinese must have exerted on the Indian president, something unusual and indicative of the highest priority that Beijing attached to OBOR. The Chinese, it should be said, very rarely threw their weight around, at least in the time I was there, and were careful with and respectful of the other four countries and of the non-Chinese in the NDB.

Even worse for the Bank than the disagreements and conflicts between India and China was the confrontation between Russia and the West arising from the crisis in Ukraine and the annexation of Crimea in 2014. Under US leadership, more than 40 countries, including all developed nations, imposed a variety of sanctions on Russia. The Russians were more than ready to rise to this challenge and have successfully resisted these pressures in the last six years. But as a result, for example, they lost access to several sources of long-term external financing, including the World Bank and the European Bank for Reconstruction and Development (EBRD). Until then, Russia was a regular recipient of World Bank loans and the main borrower from the EBRD. Since developed countries have ample majorities in these MDBs, they had no difficulty in vetoing loans to Russia.

Unexpected, however, was the behavior, at least for a certain period, of the AIIB, an institution led by China, as mentioned. All major European countries had joined AIIB, despite, I note in passing, the objections of the United States—even the UK, known for its close ties with Washington, became surprisingly the first major Western country to announce the intention of becoming a founding member of the MDB controlled by China. Just as in older multilateral institutions, the Europeans had formed a block in AIIB and began to object against any operations of the institution with Russia. Now, they did not have sufficient votes to block operations, but President Jin Liqun—so I was told by Russian representatives to the NDB—indicated at one point that he would somehow accept this veto, even if not explicitly. Russian indignation with this was so strong that something uncommon occurred. During a BRICS ministerial meeting, in Shanghai, in June 2017, with as many as about 30 persons in the room, the Russian finance minister, Anton Siluanov, directly addressing the Chinese finance minister, Jin Renquing, complained emphatically about what was going on in the AIIB, adding that this only increased Russia's reluctance to agree with membership expansion in the NDB.

In truth, the problem had started way before. As we saw, from the very beginning of the NDB's operations, Russia attempted—and would eventually succeed—in obstructing plans to bring in new countries to the Bank. The other founding members supported expansion of membership, particularly Brazil and China. India, initially in favor, began to fear that China would sponsor Pakistan's entry and lost enthusiasm for the idea, but did not actually hinder and even helped occasionally. South Africa did not seem to follow a consistent line and tended to neutrality.

Inside the Bank the propelling force was the Brazilian vice-presidency. Membership expansion was one of the matters under our responsibility, as already mentioned, and we dedicated months and months to preparation of the conditions and criteria for the admittance of new members, as well as to the work of planning and carrying out the initial rounds of contacts with the authorities of a large number of countries in 2016 and 2017. But we encountered Russian resistance all along the way. Russian representatives in the Board of Directors, aided and abetted by the Russian vice president, were always eager to please Moscow and to act according to instructions from the capital. Feeling the weakness of the president of the NDB and his reluctance to outvote or displease any of the members in the slightest manner, the Russians gradually hardened their resistance and came up with an unnerving and seemingly endless list of objections and bureaucratic maneuvers. To me, it was totally clear at time that had the president been more assertive, the Russians would not have moved into that sort of behavior and would have sought some sort of compromise with the countries favoring membership expansion.

Russians are a great and admirable people, perhaps the most interesting of the BRICS, but transparency has never been one of their strong points. At the time of the negotiations of the NDB and the CRA, as we saw above, it had never been entirely clear why they opposed, or wanted to delay, the creation of these financial mechanisms. After the establishment of the NDB, we soon felt Russia's reluctance toward new members and, again, there was no frank dialogue about this. However, with time, it became possible to surmise that there were two main reasons for this. Firstly, Russia feared the entry of its enemies in the Bank. Understandably, the objection was directed, discreetly at first, and ever more clearly over time, to the entry of developed countries, particularly those that played a prominent role in applying sanctions to Russia. This was understandable but was extended, less understandably, to small advanced countries that played a negligible part in the sanctions—the case of Switzerland and Luxemburg, for instance, countries that had indicated an interest in joining the NDB and entertained, in so far as I knew and had gathered from conversations with Russian officials, good relations with Russia.

This created something of a bind for the Brazilian vice-presidency. On the one hand, Russia objected to advanced countries. On the other hand, Treasury and some others in the NDB and in the Board of Directors feared that the entry only of EMDCs might hurt the prospects for obtaining a good credit rating for the Bank with the major international credit rating agencies. This was groundless, in my view, and poorly argued by the South African vice-presidency. The Brazilian vice-presidency demolished these arguments, but this was yet another source of delay and conflict for us.[38] To start making the NDB gradually relevant on a global scale, we had to overcome multiple obstacles—in order of importance: the Russians, the hesitations of the NDB's president, and the concerns of the South African vice president.

Secondly, to make things worse, Russia also objected, albeit less emphatically, to the admission of EMDCs, none of which (with the exception of a few emerging market countries of the European Union and, of course, Ukraine) applied any sanctions at all. The impression that the Russians conveyed was that they did not wish to compete for NDB loans with other EMDC member countries.[39] Ironically, the country that up to the beginning of 2013 had been reluctant to agree with the creation of a new bank by the BRICS now became the one most eager to use it for its own ends and meet its financing needs.

Part of the problem arose, so it seemed, from the nature of decision-making in Russia. Representatives of the country in the NDB's Board of Directors, as well as the Russian vice president, lived in the fear of displeasing the Kremlin. They had no access to the higher levels of government, and no clear idea of President Putin's views. In doubt, they did what they could do to block. In one formal Board of Directors' meeting, pressed by arguments put forward by me and some of his Board colleagues, the Russian director, Sergei Storchak, let it slip that he could not agree with the discussion of a list of possible new

38. This was done in verbal discussions and in writing. We presented detailed exercises to assess the likely effect of membership expansion, as then envisaged, on the NDB's prospective international credit rating, applying a methodology used by Moody's. The baseline scenario was the entry of 15 EMDCs, Switzerland and Luxemburg. These 17 countries had, by that time, indicated an interest (or were expected to soon do so) in beginning formal negotiations for accession to the NDB. Our conclusion was that membership expansion on this basis would bring, at best, a small positive contribution and that there was no reason to fear that it could hurt the institution's debut credit rating. See New Development Bank, *Analysis of the Impact of New Membership on NDB's Credit Rating*, Strategy and Partnerships Division and Economic Research Unit, 4th version, August 29, 2017, available at https://www.nogueirabatista.com.br/category/documentos/brics/ndb.

39. According to the Articles of Agreement, the NDB would be open to borrowing and non-borrowing members, the former being the BRICS and other EMDCs (Articles 2 and 5(c) of the AoA). Only under certain conditions could loans and other operations be made in non-member countries. For this to happen, the Board of Governors would need to approve, by special majority, a general policy in relation to projects in a non-member EMDC, subject to the condition that these projects involve a material interest of a member country, as defined by such policy (Article 19 (d) of the AoA). Subject to the same condition, the Board of Directors could exceptionally approve a specific project in a non-member EMDC, also by special majority (Article 19 (e) of the AoA). Thus, by keeping out non-BRICS EMDCs, Russian officials seemed to wish to rule out new competitors for the NDB's lending capacity.

member countries because "my Leader [Putin] is unpredictable." China, in turn, ended up accommodating Russia's objections to some extent, in part, I presume, to compensate for what was occurring in AIIB at the time, in part because in the strategic and diplomatic terrain the two countries were coming closer, as a result of China's increasing tensions with the United States, even before Donald Trump's election.

During the period I was in the NDB, we did manage to achieve some results in terms of membership expansion despite the obstacles that the Russians never tired to put forward. After some delays, we managed to obtain from the Board of Governors a go-ahead to initiate informal contacts with potentially interested countries. Throughout 2016 and 2017, we carried out several rounds of meetings with authorities of countries in Latin America, the Caribbean, Africa, the Middle East, Europe, Asia, and Oceania. I took advantage, in this process, of the experience accumulated in my more than eight years in the IMF Board and of contacts I had made in this period with finance ministers and other government officials of many countries. Interest in the NDB was uneven, but by mid-2017 more than 40 countries had indicated a desire to pursue discussions, with many of them wishing to start formal negotiations. We also managed to approve in the Board of Governors the already mentioned document that spelled out the terms, conditions, and procedures for the admission of new members. Unfortunately, the Russians immediately invented that one more document was required to establish the criteria for selection of new members—yet another pretext for delays and prolonged discussions. The truth is that the Brazilian vice-presidency worked tirelessly to achieve what were, in the end, relatively modest results. After I left the Bank, in October 2017, the process seems to have stopped completely or almost completely. Five years after its creation, no new country had joined the Bank. Meanwhile, the AIIB, created shortly after the NDB, had early on more than 90 member countries from all regions of the world, many of which were developed countries. At the end of 2019, the AIIB was the third largest MDB in the world by membership, after the World Bank and the AfDB.[40] By mid-2020, its membership included as many as 103 approved countries worldwide, including regional, non-regional, and prospective members.[41] One can only hope that the new Brazilian president, who took office in July 2020, will prove capable of finally initiating the NDB's membership expansion.

But let us return to the macro-developments that hampered the NDB's consolidation. Besides poor relations between China and India and Russia's

---

40. Humphrey, *From Drawing Board to Reality*, p. 3.
41. Counting Hong Kong, a special administrative region of China. Asian Infrastructure Investment Bank, *Members and Prospective Members of the Bank*, http//www.aiib.org.

vulnerabilities after Crimea, the Bank also came up against the fallout from the economic and political crises in South Africa and Brazil, especially in the latter. In South Africa, after a long period of political uncertainty, accusations of corruption eventually led to the resignation of President Zuma who had had a decisive role in the BRICS process, notably in the launching of the formal negotiations in the Durban Summit that led to the creation of the CRA and the NDB, as mentioned earlier in this book. I was there and can testify to the effect that without the efforts of the South Africans, President Zuma especially, it would have been probably impossible to reach in Durban the decision to create these financial mechanisms and initiate formal negotiations.

Even more important for the BRICS and for the NDB was the Brazilian crisis of 2015–16 and the impeachment of President Dilma Rousseff in August 2016. At the risk of overemphasizing the role of my country, I believe it should be said nevertheless, once again, that Brazil was more often than not the engine of the BRICS up to 2014. Although the original initiative was Russian, as we saw, Brazil more than the others stood out for its capability of formulating, organizing, and pushing the BRICS process forward. With the crisis that hit the Rousseff Administration and the economy, Brazil's ability to act underwent a clear erosion. During the Temer Administration, from mid-2016 to end-2018, the situation worsened further, and even more after Jair Bolsonaro assumed office in January 2019. Rumors that Brazil would leave the BRICS and the NDB were never plausible and nothing of the sort happened. Brazil continued to take part in the process. Since the impeachment, however, Brazil has often been simply going through the motions and the country's role declined precipitously. With Bolsonaro's policy of alignment to the Trump Administration, the situation became even more problematic, especially since at the same time China's relations with the United States took a turn for the worse. In June 2019, as the BRICS gathered with other G20 members for the G20 Leader's Summit in Osaka, Japan, the Leaders of the BRICS did meet again separately, under Bolsonaro's chairmanship, given that Brazil chaired the BRICS process in that year following the agreed rotation, and they again issued a joint statement,[42] following the tradition inaugurated in Los Cabos in 2012. A few months later, in November, they met in Brasília for their annual Summit. However, Brazil's 2019 chairmanship of the BRICS was lackluster in terms of results and content of statements, as well as absence of any initiatives to speak of. Perhaps symptomatically, the Leaders of Russia, India, and China held a separate trilateral meeting in Osaka, something that, to my knowledge, had not happened before on the sidelines of G20 meetings. The conjecture

42. *Joint Statement on BRICS Leaders' Informal Meeting on the Margins of the G20 Summit*, Osaka, Japan, June 28, 2019.

can be made that Putin, Modi, and Xi Jinping may not have felt comfortable to address some matters in the presence of Bolsonaro.

Given my identification with the Lula and Dilma Administrations, I ended up in a precarious situation after the impeachment. I no longer had the same access to or the same ease of dialogue with the Temer government and could well fear that an attempt to destabilize me in Shanghai might come from Brasília at any moment, even though I had a mandate and a contract up to 2021 and could not be removed from office *ad nutum*. About one year after the impeachment, a way was found to force me out of the Bank,[43] but it remained possible for me to work relatively well with Brasília, even during the Temer Administration, while Brazil was represented in the Board of Directors by two career diplomats, Ambassadors Luís Balduino and Carlos Cozendey, who continued initially in the positions of director and alternate director, respectively, to which they had been appointed in the Dilma Administration. These two diplomats were part of the group of Foreign Ministry officials who had played an outstanding role in the BRICS process and thus had full knowledge of what was intended with the creation of the NDB.

Toward the end of 2016, however, they were replaced by economists with little experience and knowledge pertinent to a MDB and international negotiations. Even worse, the new director for Brazil, Marcello Estevão, was full of preconceived notions and had little disposition to learn. This harmed not only Brazil's representation in the NDB but also more broadly the Board of Directors, since Brazil, by agreement reached in Fortaleza, held the first chair of this Board, as indicated above, and the Articles of Agreement had fixed the duration of this mandate at four years.[44] Formerly a mid-level member of IMF staff, with permanent residence in and strong links to the United States, the new Brazilian representative soon proved his inaptitude for the position, displaying behavior that smacked of amateurism and improvisation. With naive frankness, he revealed skepticism, perhaps even hostility, to the NDB

43. I explained the methods used to remove me from office in *O Brasil não cabe no quintal de ninguém*, pp. 284–87; and also in a short paper I prepared at the time of my departure from Shanghai, "Note on the situation of the New Development Bank, and the treatment given to the Brazilian Vice President," October 15, 2017, pp. 4 and 5, https://www.nogueirabatista.com.br/category/documentos/brics/ndb/. What occurred was illegal in the sense that my mandate and contract were violated. Jonnas Esmeraldo Marques de Vasconcelos, *BRICS: Agenda regulatória*. 2018. Tese (Doutorado)—Faculdade de Direito da Universidade de São Paulo, São Paulo, 2018, https://bdpi.usp.br/item/002910177, pp. 183–94, provides a detailed account of the matter, presenting my dismissal as an example of "lawfare" at an administrative level and including many of the pertinent internal documents (annexes B, C, D, E, and F).

44. Article 12 (d) of the AoA.

as a project. For instance, at a formal meeting of the Board of Directors in Shanghai, he caused perplexity by stating, out of the blue, that the NDB, having been created during the Dilma Administration, would have been a hard sell had it been proposed to the Temer Administration. Sometime later, at a BRICS deputies meeting, in Washington, DC, he complained about a proposal made by the Chinese, and taken up by the Administration of the NDB, to produce an economic report for the BRICS Summit in Xiamen, arguing that IMF reports were more than enough.[45] I still remember the surprised look of the Chinese officials, not used to hearing that sort of talk from Brazilian representatives. Unfortunately, this was the type of person that came to be the norm for Brazil from mid-2016 onward. In Brasília, the tone was set from then on by economists and other professionals that, while not necessarily as naive and amateurish as the Brazilian director in the NDB, had little or no identification with the BRICS process. Their loyalty was, generally speaking, to the United States and, in particular, to the Bretton Woods institutions—the IMF and the World Bank.

The NDB achieves results but fails to live up to expectations

All these political setbacks with the capitals were difficult to face but not unsurmountable or unprecedented. Multilateral organizations encounter such challenges now and then, arising from political and economic problems in their larger member countries. To deal with them, however, an indispensable ingredient was missing in the NDB: an Administration—and especially a president—strongly dedicated, willing to struggle and run certain risks. In the absence of this ingredient, the NDB obtained some results but evolved slowly and accumulated a number of failures, some of which I have already commented on.

The main goal of the Bank, it must be remembered, is to support projects in the areas of infrastructure and sustainable development. On this crucial matter, achievements were unsatisfactory in the institution's first five years. The NDB found ways to disguise this, and so a close look at the available information is required to understand what actually happened.

In its public communication, the NDB usually stresses the approval of projects by the Board of Directors. In the first five years, up to June 2020, 57 projects were approved in a total amount of approximately US$ 18 billion.[46]

45. For some details on the background of this official, especially his links to the United States, see Nogueira Batista Jr., "Note on the Situation of the New Development Bank," pp. 3 and 4.

46. New Development Bank, *Investor Presentation*, August 2020, p. 20, http//www.ndb.int. Or 55 projects, totaling about US$ 17.7 billion, excluding two projects that were

China obtained 29 percent of approvals, India 28 percent, South Africa 18 percent, Russia 16 percent, and Brazil 9 percent.[47] The higher amounts for China and India are presumably not unrelated to the fact that India held the first presidency and that the NDB's headquarters are in China. Loan approvals accelerated in the final semester of Kamath's presidency because of lending related to the COVID-19 crisis. The NDB, as all other MDBs, jumped to show usefulness in combating the pandemic and its Board approved large and vaguely defined program loans for all member countries, except Russia.[48]

At first sight, this amount of loan approvals might seem a good result for a relatively new bank. Appearances deceive, however. Even in China and India, the NDB's presence is actually minimal. This is because the approval of a project by directors is only a step in its implementation, and not necessarily the most difficult one. After Board approval, contracts have to be negotiated and signed and, subsequently, disbursements have to be made. Now, project documents approved by directors are, normally, of a generic nature and often postpone the solution of thorny issues. Therefore, the negotiation and signing of contracts can take a long time, as mostly happens. In some cases, contracts are never completed, and projects approved by the Board become skeletons in the wardrobe, without however being removed from the NDB's list of approvals.[49] Perhaps more importantly, even when contracts are signed, as happens in most cases, disbursements occur with great delay. Thus, the NDB's speed, highlighted in the Bank's strategy, is doubtlessly a fiction, including in the critical field of project financing and other operations. The Bank has been slow and has had little impact in its five member countries.

Embarrassing for the NDB is the fact that, after five years of existence, total disbursements reached only US$ 2.2 billion.[50] There was progress in terms of

---

approved by the Board but subsequently cancelled. New Development Bank, *Annual Report 2019—Investing for Innovation*, pp. 6 and 7, http//www.ndb.int.

47. New Development Bank, *Investor Presentation*, p. 20.

48. Brazil, India, and South Africa obtained Board approval for emergency COVID-related program lending of US$ 1 billion each. China obtained a RMB 7 billon loan (equivalent to about US$ 1 billion). New Development Bank, *New Development Bank COVID-19 Response Programme*, http//www.ndb.int. The information provided on these program loans is scanty.

49. However, the NDB's Annual Report, as indicated in footnote 98, refers to the cancellation of two projects of the list, one in India, a US$ 250 million loan to a state-owned bank, the other in Russia, a US$ 69 million loan for a road. New Development Bank, *Annual Report 2019*, pp. 6 and 7. It is quite possible that other projects in the list of approvals will eventually be cancelled.

50. New Development Bank, *Investor Presentation*, p. 34. The amount of disbursements referred to in the text corresponds to loans and advances as of March 31, 2020. This is a reasonable approximation of the accumulated disbursements in the first years, given

disbursement in the last two years[51] but this was due largely, if not exclusively, to disbursements made under loans to national development institutions or other national financial intermediaries and, in particular, to disbursements under program loans, notably COVID-related emergency financing.[52] In these cases, disbursements are much easier but the NDB's presence in the field is actually limited or nonexistent, given that project or program implementation is carried out entirely, or almost entirely, by other entities.

Even so, disbursements fell short of the scenarios outlined in the NDB's General Strategy, and the same can be said, to a lesser extent, of loan approvals. In that document, the amount of cumulative loan disbursements, under assumptions presented as conservative, was expected to reach a much higher value, between US$ 8.75 billion and US$ 10.8 billion by end-2020.[53] Cumulative loans approvals were expected to reach between US$ 22 billion and US$ 29.5 billion.[54]

An ambitious and expensive plan of creating an MDB of global reach has petered out into a five-member bank that basically receives capital from members, makes small disbursements, pays staff and operational expenditures, and deposits excess resources in well-reputed financial institutions and in other safe and low-return venues. A far cry, of course, from what we originally intended in the BRICS process. The picture may change in the future—and I hope it does—but, unfortunately, this is the reality of the Bank in its first five years.

Another goal that was achieved only partially was that of operating with the national currencies of member countries. Only for the Chinese currency

---

that the great majority of loans is denominated in US dollars (meaning that valuation changes linked to exchange rate fluctuations are small) and that little or no payments of principal occurred in this period due to the long grace periods foreseen in the loan contracts.

51. In its first three years, the NDB had disbursed, believe it or not, only US$ 226 million (loans and advances as of June 30, 2018). New Development Bank, *Investor Presentation*, October 2018, p. 23, http//www.ndb.int.
52. For instance, the emergency assistance loan to India of US$ 1 billion was fully disbursed on May 11, 2020, eleven days after Board approval. New Development Bank, "NDB Fully Disbursed Emergency Assistance Program Loan to India to Fight COVID-19 Related Outbreak," Press Release, May 12, 2020, http//www.ndb.int. The Bank's policy for this type of lending allows disbursement of up to 100 percent of the loan in one installment upon request of the borrower. New Development Bank, *Policy on Fast-Track Emergency Response to COVID-19*, approved June 10, 2020, paragraph 18, http//www.ndb.int.
53. New Development Bank, *NDB's General Strategy: 2017–2021*, tables 2 and 3, pp. 18 and 19.
54. Ibid.

were significant results accomplished. Up to mid-2020, out of the 57 loans approved, 10 projects, totaling US$ 3.6 billion, are denominated in Chinese renminbis, and 4 projects in South African rands, totaling US$ 1.1 billion.[55] Nothing was done in the currencies of the other three member countries, despite repeated announcements of intention. As much as 74 percent of the total amount of approved loans are denominated in hard currencies, of which 67 percent are in US dollars, 4 percent in euros, and 3 percent in Swiss francs; the remaining 26 percent are in national currencies of member countries, of which 20 percent in renminbis and 6 percent in rands.[56]

Moreover, it took the Bank many years to return to capital markets after 2016. After the successful but small first issuance in July 2016, nothing more occurred for a number of years. *Et pour cause*: there was no need. Founding members brought in paid-in capital as scheduled in the Articles of Agreement, some even anticipating installments. With disbursements at modest levels, why go back to capital markets? Of course, this paralysis had its price: the NDB took a long time to begin to create a name in the market and staff did not gain practical experience with bond issuance. Partly for the same reason, the NDB took as long as three years to obtain an international credit rating. The result was not bad (AA+), but below the triple A obtained by all main MDBs, including AIIB.[57] Only in February 2019 did the NDB tap the markets again by issuing another small bond for RMB 3 billion (equivalent to US$ 448 million at the date of issuance), of which RMB 2 billion were for three years and RMB 1 billion for five years, with coupon rates of 3 percent and 3.32 percent, respectively.[58] The operation

---

55. New Development Bank, *List of All Projects.*
56. New Development Bank, *Investor Presentation*, August 2020, p. 20. The NDB also made little progress in operations with the private sector or without sovereign guarantees. In the first five years, non-sovereign operations accounted for only 10 percent of total approvals. New Development Bank, *Investor Presentation*, August 2020, p. 20.
57. The NDB obtained AA+ from S&P and Fitch. A triple A international rating was granted by two less important agencies: Japan Credit Rating Agency and Analytic Credit Rating Agency (a Russian institution). Two Chinese agencies, as well as the Russian agency, granted the NDB a triple A domestic credit rating. New Development Bank, *Investor Presentation*, August 20, p. 16. It would have been difficult to match the result of the AIIB that had a great number and variety of members, including all main advanced countries, with the exception of the United States and Japan. The NDB's small membership implies concentration of portfolio and risks. And the absence of developed countries also hampered the obtention of a triple A from the major international credit rating agencies.
58. New Development Bank, *Annual Report 2019*, pp. 55 and 74.

seems to have been successful, presumably with strong support from China again.[59]

After that, issuance activity picked up considerably, with the NDB taking advantage of the abundant liquidity in international and domestic markets. In April 2020, the Bank issued a larger bond, called Coronavirus Combating Bond, this time for RMB 5 billion (the equivalent of approximately US$ 700 million) with a 3-year tenor at a 2.43 percent annual coupon rate.[60] In 2019 and the first half of 2020, a series of short-term notes were issued to enhance liquidity management.[61] And in June 2020, the NDB priced a 3-year bond for US$ 1.5 billion in international capital markets, also linked to the funding of COVID-related program loans.[62]

The NDB's lack of transparency should also be noted. Information on the Bank's projects is very limited, making it impossible to check from the outside whether the NDB is respecting, in practice, the principles established in the Articles of Agreement, in the General Strategy, and in the interviews and speeches of the Administration. In so far as I know, there has been no definition of how to operationalize and monitor the strategy's focus on sustainable infrastructure. Nor is it known, concretely, how the NDB acts in each project to ensure respect for environmental and social sustainability. Little can be learned about the approved projects in the NDB's web page and in the Bank's official documents.[63]

---

59. The bond was oversubscribed three times its offer book. New Development Bank, *Annual Report 2019*, pp. 4 and 55.
60. New Development Bank, *Annual Report 2019*, pp. 7 and 127. This bond is intended to support the financing of public health expenditures in Hubei, Guandong, and Henan, the provinces hardest hit by COVID-19. The proceeds of the issuance are expected to be fully utilized in the above-mentioned RMB 7 billion emergency assistance program loan to China approved by the NDB's Board in March 2020. New Development Bank, "New Development Bank Issues Coronavirus Combating Bond Raising RMB 5 Billion", *Press Release*, April 3, 2020, http//www.ndb.int.
61. New Development Bank, *Annual Report 2019*, pp. 13, 121, 127. In this period, the NDB also established bond issuance programs for international markets, as well as in China, South Africa, and Russia. New Development Bank, *Annual Report 2019*, pp. 4, 79.
62. The coupon rate was 0.625 percent. Central banks and official institutions (not specified by the NDB) accounted for 75 percent of the allocations. New Development Bank, "NDB Prices Inaugural USD 1.5 Billion 3-Year COVID Response Bond in International Capital Markets", *Press Release*, June 17, 2020, http//www.ndb.int.
63. Available information, not more than a few paragraphs per project, can be found in the list of projects in the NDB's web page. New Development Bank, *List of All Projects*. As mentioned previously, the large loans approved for COVID-related purposes, for instance, are described superficially by short summaries. New Development Bank, *New Development Bank COVID-19 Response Programme*.

There is also little or no information about other relevant aspects of the institution's activities, for instance on hiring of staff. No information is provided on how or whether the positions of director generals and chief were filled.[64] A good question to be asked to the Bank is how many of these positions have been filled and by whom, including information on the breakdown by gender and nationality. When I left the NDB in late 2017 many of these remained vacant—another example of the Bank's slowness.

***

The first five years of the NDB were, in short, a disappointment. An institution that had initially generated curiosity, interest, as well as concern in some quarters, and that presented seemingly promising results in the beginning, faced all sorts of internal and macro-problems and soon crystallized into a sideshow. Under K. V. Kamath, the NDB did not really take off. It evolved slowly and hesitantly, with a weak Administration and a staff of uneven quality. It remained well below the ambitious original design that foresaw the establishment of a global MDB, modern, innovative, and technically solid.

A new Administration, under a Brazilian president, and with the foreseen replacement of all vice presidents by mid-2021, holds the promise of a renewal. It can be hoped that Russia, India, and South Africa will be more successful in the second round of appointments of its nationals for the crucial positions of vice presidents, compensating, at least in part, for a possible insufficiency of the Brazilian president. It would probably also be necessary to replace part of the director generals and chiefs and to fill in vacant staff positions.

A turnaround is certainly possible. After all, the NDB is there and has achieved, even if slowly, some significant results. Capital has been paid-in, a number of projects and program loans have been approved, favorable credit ratings were obtained, disbursements and bond issuances have picked up since 2019, and nearly 150 people were employed fulltime as of end-2019.[65] The Bank has only begun and undoubtedly still has great potential. We should not abandon the hope that all the efforts that were put in to creating this institution will come to fruition sooner or later.

---

64. Up to the end of 2020, the NDB's organization structure foresaw 16 director generals and 22 chiefs. New Development Bank, *NDB Organisation Structure*, available at https://www.nogueirabatista.com.br/category/documentos/brics/ndb/. In December 2020, the Board approved a new organization structure that increased the number of director generals to 21 and that of chiefs to 28. New Development Bank, *Organizational Structure*, http//www.ndb.int.
65. New Development Bank, *Annual Report 2019*, p. 60.

Chapter 5

WHITHER THE BRICS? FINAL CONSIDERATIONS

A sense of disappointment permeates this book, or at least parts of it. But, as mentioned in the introduction, this is to some extent a consequence of the perhaps excessive ambition that people like me had at the outset of the BRICS process in 2008 and, especially, when the CRA and NDB, after difficult negotiations, were successfully launched in Fortaleza in July 2014. Nevertheless, looking at the big picture and trying to imagine things to come, I believe it is safe to say that the BRICS are here to stay. Cooperation between the five countries is likely to continue uninterrupted, with ups and downs of course, but sufficiently strong to decisively affect their international relations and the balance of power in an increasingly multipolar world. Not only is the development bank something unique in the history of our countries, but the BRICS process as a whole should be seen and valued from this angle—as the unprecedented transregional joining of forces of nations with different features and histories but united by common strategic purposes.

Since the creation of the BRICS, China's relative political and economic importance has increased continuously—in the world and relatively to the other BRICS countries. The group has become more lopsided than it originally was and, on present trends, will become even more so in the future. However, a point I made about my experience in Shanghai—that the Chinese very rarely threw their weight around and were respectful of the other four countries—can be made more broadly about China's behavior in the BRICS process as a whole.

In any case, the other four countries will undoubtedly continue to have a significant weight. India, in particular, also accounts for a rising share of the world's economy and, even more than China, of the world's population. Russia has demonstrated, time and again, its capacity to act independently and vigorously in several regions of the world. The country is respected and even feared. South Africa will continue to hold the key to events in sub-Saharan Africa. Brazil, currently at its nadir, will sooner or later again play the constructive and independent role the world is accustomed to see.

One can expect China to retain a lasting interest in BRICS cooperation—even more so if relations with the United States remain fraught with tensions, as seems likely. Something similar can be said of Russia. The country's confrontation with the West over issues such as Ukraine and Crimea had an ambiguous effect for the BRICS. On the one hand, it favored the process, by making Russia even more interested in cooperating with the other four countries, especially China. On the other hand, it weakened the main concrete result of the BRICS—the NDB—by delaying for several years the entry of new countries into the Bank. But one can hope that this barrier shall be overcome and that the NDB will not take long to initiate expansion of membership, even if slowly.[1] The fact that the president of the institution is now a Brazilian may help in this regard, for Brazil, together with China, was always the country most interested in promoting the entry of new members into the Bank.

Should the BRICS formation itself expand to include other EMDCs? This is a completely different matter, not addressed in this book. It comes up now and then, with China being the main, if not exclusive, proponent of the idea, sometimes referred to as BRICS+. The other countries are somewhere between reluctant and opposed to BRICS+ on the grounds that expansion might weaken the cohesion and effectiveness of the group and also, perhaps mainly, out of fear that new countries, being necessarily smaller than the four original members, might kowtow to China, further accentuating the lopsidedness of the group. Moreover, it should not be forgotten that the BRICS formation, similar to other groupings of this kind, such as the G20 or the G7, works on the basis of consensus, meaning that in theory each member can block statements or decisions. In practice, it is difficult to do so on an individual basis, and especially to do so repeatedly, but if a country feels strongly about any issue and has some capacity to articulate support, it can garner

1. The BRICS Leaders, in their 2019 Summit in Brasília, referred to the matter in the following terms: "We acknowledge the progress made by the New Development Bank towards expanding its membership. The expansion of the NDB membership in accordance with its Articles of Agreement will strengthen the Bank's role as a global development finance institution and further contribute to the mobilization of resources for infrastructure and sustainable development projects in BRICS and other EMDCs. We look forward to the Board of Governors concluding the preparatory work with the aim of taking timely and considered decisions on the expansion of the membership in due course." *Eleventh BRICS Summit—Brasília Declaration*, Brasília, Brazil, November 14, 2019, paragraph 32. A positive statement, even if still vague. A year later, in their Summit in Moscow, the Leaders welcomed the beginning of formal negotiations with potential candidates for membership without providing further information. *Twelfth BRICS Summit—Moscow Declaration*, Moscow, Russia, November 17. 2020, paragraph 60.

a significant minority to oppose specific statements or decisions.[2] Thus an increase in the number of members can weaken the group's decision-making process and even bring the risk of paralysis.

This problem does not arise, at least not in the same manner, with an expansion of the CRA or of the NDB. Consensus is not generally adopted as a rule for decision-making in these bodies, more clearly in the case of the Articles of Agreement of the NDB where no decision requires unanimity. For reasons indicated in Chapters 3 and 4 of this book, expansion of both financing mechanisms, and especially of the NDB, would be advisable—expansion in terms of the number of member countries, as well as in the amount of paid-in capital of the NDB or of the size of the arrangement in the case of the CRA. The NDB, as we saw, has an egalitarian distribution of capital and voting power among the five founding members. Furthermore, the Articles of Agreement of the NDB do not allow the voting power of the founding members to fall below 55 percent of total voting power, with each of them retaining at least 11 percent.[3] The institution will thus remain in the hands of its founding members.

While increasing the number of countries around the table, at the political level of the BRICS formation, could enhance the group's influence, on balance it would seem preferable to keep it as a five-country initiative, but taking up again and strengthening the practice of regional outreach—a practice abandoned by the Bolsonaro Administration in its presidency of the BRICS in 2019. Regional outreach worked well in the Durban and Fortaleza summits, for instance, with South Africa and Brazil inviting the Leaders of the countries from sub-Saharan Africa and South America to take part in the last day of the Summit and meet the BRICS leaders for a face-to-face dialogue. It worked less well in the Xiamen Summit in 2017, when China tried, not very successfully, to go for a global outreach and invite the Leaders of countries from different regions of the world, a decision that reflected perhaps the tensions in Asia, and in particular disagreements between China and India. Similar difficulties in South and Latin America, possibly worse than the ones faced by China, led Brazil to shy away from a regional outreach in the Brasília Summit in 2019—a reflection of the decline of Brazilian prestige

2. For a discussion of the functioning of consensus-based groups, such as the G20 and the BRICS, see Paulo Nogueira Batista Jr., *O Brasil não cabe no quintal de ninguém: bastidores da vida de um economista brasileiro no FMI e nos BRICS e outros textos sobre nacionalismo e nosso complexo de vira-lata*, São Paulo, LeYa, 2019, pp. 36–37 and 72–78.
3. Article 8 (c, i) of the AoA. The total voting power of non-borrowing countries (advanced economies) cannot exceed 20 percent of the total. Article 8 (c, ii). The individual share of a non-founding member cannot exceed 7 percent. Article 8 (c, iii).

in its regional environment during the Temer and, especially, the Bolsonaro governments.

The likes of Temer and Bolsonaro are hopefully a temporary departure from Brazil's long-standing autonomous or at least relatively autonomous international policy. There is in Brazil a strong streak—"tradition" would perhaps not be too strong a word—of independence and non-alignment with the United States and other Western powers. In this respect, the Lula and Dilma Administrations stand out, but it was also to some extent a part of previous Administrations, including during the military regime, notably in the Geisel Administration (1974–79). Despite insistent rumors to the contrary, even Temer and Bolsonaro—if only for the rather narrow reason that the BRICS are seen as an avenue of cooperation with China, the country's main trading partner—did not move away from the BRICS process and the financial mechanisms they created, although Brazil's participation lost drive and content.

I attempted to describe the origins of the group and the skepticism with which the viability of BRICS cooperation was seen at first. Indeed, the five countries have diverse interests and form a diverse group. However, there is one key aspect that was (and is) common to all, especially the four original members—we are large and important nations whose interests and views were (and still are) largely ignored, or at least not taken into due account. If only for this reason, cooperation between the BRICS is likely to continue for a long time. It will of course be subject to ups and downs, as mentioned, reflecting mostly the changing political and economic circumstances in the five countries and in their international relations. Throughout the book I avoided referring to the BRICS as a "bloc" or an "alliance," choosing instead to use expressions as "cooperation mechanism," "group," or "formation." Another expression or analogy, perhaps more appropriate, would be to refer to the BRICS as a "club," with members that share certain important common interests, but are otherwise fully independent.

Whatever the expression preferred, "club," "formation," or "cooperation mechanism," the BRICS can be expected to continue to work together on strategically significant political and economic matters and to have a major role for our countries and in the world in the years to come.

REFERENCES

Official documents

ASEAN + 3 Macroeconomic Research Office. *Governance—Executive Committee*, https://www.amro-asia.org/about-amro/who-we-are/executive-committee/.

Asian Development Bank. *Chiang Mai Initiative [Mulitaleralization]*, Asia Regional Integration Center: Tracking Asian Integration, https://aric.adb.org/initiative/chiang-mai-initiative.

Asian Infrastructure Investment Bank. *Members and Prospective Members of the Bank*, http://www.aiib.org.

BRIC. *Second BRIC Summit of Heads of State and Government—Joint Statement*, Brasília, April 15, 2010.

BRICS. "BRICS Leaders' Announcement on Reserve Pooling and Currency Swap Arrangements", draft, Los Cabos, Mexico, June 18, 2012, https://www.nogueirabatista.com.br/category/documentos/brics/cra/.

BRICS. "Media note on the informal meeting of BRICS Leaders ahead of the G20 Summit in Los Cabos", Los Cabos, Mexico, June 18, 2012.

BRICS. *Statement of the BRICS Leaders on the Establishment of the BRICS-Led Development Bank*, Durban, South Africa, March 27, 2013.

BRICS. *BRICS CRA*, Working Group Meeting, Washington, DC, October 8, 2013, https://www.nogueirabatista.com.br/category/documentos/brics/cra/.

BRICS. *Contingent Reserve Arrangement (CRA)—Impacto para o Brasil*, Office of the Executive Director—Paulo Nogueira Batista Jr., OEDBR, International Monetary Fund, Washington, DC, October 20, 2013, https://www.nogueirabatista.com.br/category/documentos/brics/cra.

BRICS. *Agreed Minutes of the BRICS Ministerial Meeting*, Fortaleza, Brazil, July 15, 2014.

BRICS. *Articles of Agreement of the New Development Bank*, Fortaleza, Brazil, July 15, 2014.

BRICS. *Sixth BRICS Summit—Fortaleza Declaration*, Fortaleza, Brazil, July 15, 2014.

BRICS. *Treaty for the Establishment of the BRICS Contingent Arrangement*, Fortaleza, Brazil, July 15, 2014.

BRICS. *Ninth BRICS Summit—BRICS Leaders' Xiamen Declaration*, Xiamen, China, September 4, 2017.

BRICS. *Joint Statement on BRICS Leaders' Informal Meeting on the Margins of the G20 Summit*, Osaka, Japan, June 28, 2019.

BRICS. *Eleventh BRICS Summit—Brasília Declaration*, Brasília, Brazil, November 14, 2019.

BRICS. *Twelfth BRICS Summit—Moscow Declaration*, Moscow, Russia, November 17, 2020.

International Monetary Fund. *Preliminary Discussions on a Constituency-Based Plurilateral Financing Arrangement (PFA)*, Power Point Presentation, Office of the Executive Director (OEDBR),

International Monetary Fund, Technical Meeting, IMF headquarters, Washington, DC, September 11, 2013, https://www.nogueirabatista.com.br/category/documentos/fmi/.
International Monetary Fund. "PFA—Nota Pres Tombini," OEDBR, Washington, DC, 2013, https://www.nogueirabatista.com.br/category/documentos/fmi/.
Mantega, Guido. *Statement to the 18th Meeting of the IMFC*, Washington, DC, October 2008.
New Development Bank. *NDB's General Strategy: 2017–2021*, http://www.ndb.int/.
New Development Bank. *Organizational Structure*, http://www.ndb.int/.
New Development Bank. *NDB Organisation Structure Up to December 2020*, https://www.nogueirabatista.com.br/category/documentos/brics/ndb.
New Development Bank. *Terms, Conditions and Procedures for the Admission of New Members*, http://www.ndb.int/.
New Development Bank. *Analysis of the Impact of New Membership on NDB's Credit Rating*, Strategy & Partnerships Division and Economic Research Unit, 4th version, August 29, 2017, https://www.nogueirabatista.com.br/category/documentos/brics/ndb.
New Development Bank. *Investor Presentation*, October 2018, http://www.ndb.int/.
New Development Bank. *Annual Report 2019: Investing for Innovation*, http://www.ndb.int/.
New Development Bank. "New Development Bank issues Coronavirus Combating Bond raising RMB 5 billion," *Press Release*, April 3, 2020, http://www.ndb.int/.
New Development Bank. "NDB fully disbursed Emergency Assistance Program Loan to India to fight COVID-19 related outbreak", *Press Release*, May 12, 2020, http://www.ndb.int/.
New Development Bank. *Policy on Fast-Track Emergency Response to COVID-19*, approved June 10, 2020, http://www.ndb.int/.
New Development Bank. "NDB prices inaugural USD 1.5 billion 3-year COVID Response Bond in international capital markets," *Press Release*, June 17, 2020, http://www.ndb.int/.
New Development Bank. *New Development Bank COVID-19 Response Programme*, http://www.ndb.int/.
New Development Bank. *Investor Presentation*, August 2020, http://www.ndb.int/.
New Development Bank. *List of All Projects*, http://www.ndb.int/.

Other

Acioly da Silva, Luciana. *Arquitetura Financeira Conjunta do BRICS: O Novo Banco de Desenvolvimento*, Texto para Discussão 2463, Instituto de Pesquisa Econômica Aplicada—IPEA, Rio de Janeiro, March 2019.
Harrod, Roy. *The Life of John Maynard Keynes*. New York: W.W. Norton, 1982 (first edition: 1951).
Humphrey, Christopher. *Infrastructure Finance in the Developing World: Challenges and Opportunities for Multilateral Development Banks in 21st Century Infrastructure Finance*, Intergovernmental Group of Twenty-Four & Global Green Growth Institute, Working Paper Series, June 2015.
Humphrey, Christopher. *From Drawing Board to Reality: The First Four Years of Operations of the Asian Infrastructure Investment Bank and New Development Bank*, Working Paper of the G-24 & Global Development Policy Center of Boston University, April 2020.
Marques de Vasconcelos, Jonnas Esmeraldo. *BRICS: Agenda regulatória*. 2018. Tese (Doutorado)—Faculdade de Direito da Universidade de São Paulo, São Paulo, 2018, https://bdpi.usp.br/item/002910177.

Martinez-Diaz, Leonardo. *Executive Boards in International Organizations: Lessons for Strengthening IMF Governance.* Independent Evaluation Office of the IMF, IEO Background Paper, BP/08/08, revised May 2008.

Nogueira Batista Jr., Paulo. "The IMF, capital account regulation, and emerging economies," in Kevin P. Gallagher, Stephany Griffith-Jones & José Antonio Ocampo (co-chairs), *Regulating Capital Flows for Long-un Development*, Pardee Center Task Force Report, University, 2012.

Nogueira Batista Jr., Paulo. "Note on the situation of the New Development Bank, and the treatment given to the Brazilian Vice President," October 15, 2017, https://www.nogueirabatista.com.br/category/documentos/brics/ndb/.

Nogueira Batista Jr., Paulo. *O Brasil não cabe no quintal de ninguém: bastidores da vida de um economista brasileiro no FMI e nos BRICS e outros textos sobre nacionalismo e nosso complexo de vira-lata*, São Paulo, LeYa, 2019.

Stern, Nicholas. *NDB—Origins, Opportunities and Challenges*, prepared with Amar Bhattacharya, London School of Economics and Political Science / Grantham Research Institute for Climate Change and the Environment, March 2016, https://www.nogueirabatista.com.br/category/documentos/brics/ndb/.

INDEX OF NAMES

An 'n' after the page number indicates that the name was mentioned in a footnote.

www.ingramcontent.com/pod-product-compliance
Ingram Content Group UK Ltd.
Pitfield, Milton Keynes, MK11 3LW, UK
UKHW041832100926
8556IPUK00002B/129

9 781839 982064